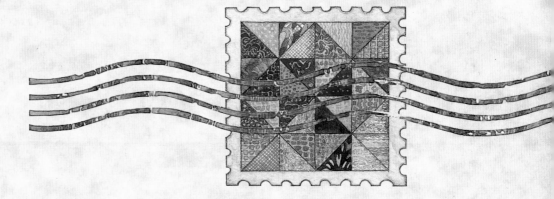

Beth Donaldson

CHARM QUILTS

*Or too much fun
with a stack of
squares and one
template!*

Published in the United States of America by EZ Quilting by Wrights.

Editing by Mary Coyne Penders.

Technical editing by Darlene Zimmerman.

Book and cover design by Kajun Graphics, San Francisco.

Stamp illustrations by Emanuel Schongut, San Francisco.

Diagrams by Kandy Petersen, Moraga, California.

Photography by Sharon Risedorph, San Francisco.

Author's photograph by Raymond D. Kopen, East Lansing, Michigan.

Printed in China

First Edition / Eighth Printing

Library of Congress Cataloguing-in-Publication Data

    1. Quilting—Charm Quilts   2. Quilting Patterns   3. Quilting—Crafts and Hobbies

    Donaldson, Beth, 1957–

ISBN 1-881588-19-X

Publisher
P.O. Box 398
West Warren, MA 01092-0398
visit www.wrights.com &
www.ezquilt.com

Table of Contents

Acknowledgments

My thanks to Pepper Cory, for hours of encouragement, guidance, sharing and friendship; to Mary Coyne Penders and Darlene Zimmerman, heroines of good grammar and consistency; to designer Pat Koren, for visually finding the heart of my book; to Kandy Petersen, who faithfully illustrated every pressing arrow in the instructions; to Sharon Risedorph, whose photographs make each quilt sing; and to Chuck Sabosik, who carried the project through leadership transitions.

Thanks to the charm quilters you'll meet in the following pages, who were generous with their time, talents and quilts. Thanks to the quilters around the world who have shared stories, patterns, blocks, fabrics and recipes!

Special thanks to my family: my sister Mary Ellen, my best press agent, who is always there to listen; my daughter Colleen, who reminds me of what's really important; my daughter Katy, whose wit and independence are inspiring; and my husband Tom, my best friend, who tolerates my ever-growing fabric collection and unusual attachment to office supplies. I love you all!

To the members of the
Capitol City Quilt Guild.
Your talent and friendship are
responsible for this book.

Introduction

CHARM QUILTS are one-patch designs with each patch cut from a different fabric. The charm quilt idea developed from the button collecting fad of the late nineteenth century, when young girls collected and traded buttons to make a button string. During the 1870s, button strings were known as charm strings. One romantic myth associated with charm strings involved collecting 999 different buttons. After this goal was achieved, the girl's true love came along with the 1000th button on his coat and the couple lived happily ever after. Much was written about button strings, but few survive, whereas very little was written about charm quilts but many survive.

Pat Nickols is an avid collector and researcher of charm quilts. Her paper, "Charm Quilts: Characteristics and Variations: 1870s-1990s," published by the American Quilt Study Group in *Uncoverings, 1996*, describes methods of fabric collecting for antique charm quilts, including trading among friends, soliciting for fabric pen pals in periodicals, buying manufacturers' sample swatches and using leftover dressmaking scraps. These methods are shared by charm quilters today.

Other common threads are the memories invoked by charm quilts, which are a rich history of friends, trips and clothing, as well as a showcase for fabric trends from the marketplace. Whether speaking of contemporary or antique charm quilts, charm quiltmakers share a love of reminiscing about where they acquired fabrics, from whom they received them, and from what garments they were gleaned.

Included in this book are thirteen different traditional one-patch templates. All the featured quilts are one-patch designs, but research shows charm quilts made with two and three-patch designs as well. A trend begun in the 1920s alternated the charm shapes with muslin or another fabric. This less random approach placed more emphasis on the quilt design.

Two important sources of inspiration for the 1980s revival of charm quilts are Jinny Beyer's book *The Scrap Look*, and Cuesta Benberry's companion articles, "Charm Quilts" (March, 1980) and "Charm Quilts Revisited" (January and February, 1988) for *Quilter's Newsletter Magazine*. These articles feature photographs of beautiful charm quilts in rich vibrant colors. Jinny's book contains templates for many one-patch designs and an entire chapter devoted to charm quilts. These sources inspired me to join a charm exchange group started by fellow quilt guild member Georgia Hayden.

The following pages will inspire you to trade fabrics with friends near and far, use your own fabrics exclusively or work from a theme. These quilts are fun, evocative, and a never to be forgotten quilting experience. Each charm quilt is a unique journey and expression of the quilt-maker's artistry.

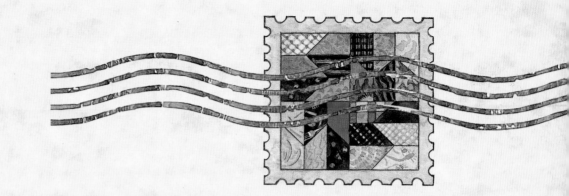

Part One

COLLECTING
FABRICS

HE MAIN GOAL of a charm quilt is never to repeat a fabric. Those of us who have been collecting fabrics for a long time can achieve this goal within our own quilt cupboards. For beginning quilters, collecting the large number of fabrics may seem challenging, but you are in for a real treat. Collecting and trading for charm squares is fun, interactive and a great chance for making new friends.

In interviewing the quiltmakers for this book, I found we all had one thing in common. These quilts have lives of their own! Charm quilting is not an exact science. No matter how well you plan, it is impossible to know just how much of one color or another you will need. When collecting fabrics, relax and enjoy the process. Try not to get too bogged down in decisions on what you think you need or what plan you want to follow. During the piecing phase, most quilters end up searching for more colors they weren't aware they needed during the collecting phase.

The more research I did, the more outlets I found for charm quilt squares. I'll be describing exchanges in local groups, pen-pal and mail swaps, e-mail and computer swapping, mail-order swatch purchasing, quilt shop purchasing and charm games held at guild meetings or symposiums.

Most charm squares come in 4″, 5″ or 6″ squares. All the templates can be cut from a 5″ x 5″ charm square. Many can be cut from a 4″ x 4″ charm square. I prefer the 5″ squares because you can center a motif more easily. Sometimes you can obtain two charm shapes from one square.

The best part of exchanging with others is receiving fabrics that you wouldn't normally buy. It's an exciting challenge to incorporate the multitude of styles now available on the market. Charm exchanges are full of pleasant surprises and new friendships.

CHARM EXCHANGE GROUPS

My own exchange group is an offshoot of the Capitol City Quilt Guild of Lansing, Michigan. The first year the guild numbered about thirty quilters. The cozy atmosphere made it easy to make friends, ask questions and share our love of quiltmaking. After four years the group had grown tremendously. Growth had its advantages: money to hire nationally known teachers and plenty of volunteers to put on fabulous quilt shows. Growth also had its downside. Business took up more of our meeting time, giving us less time to work on projects and socialize.

To re-establish friendliness and collect charm squares, Georgia Hayden organized our guild's first small group, *The Charmers*. Almost all the quiltmakers featured in the following pages are part of that first group or one of its offshoots, the *Daughters of Charm*, the *Granddaughters of Charm*, and the *Charming Offspring*. To date there have been more than six groups that began as charm exchanges.

The small group idea caught on so big with the guild that it inspired Ruth Dukelow to share her experiences by writing "Putting the 'Bee' Back in Quiltmaking" for *Quilter's Newsletter Magazine* (April, 1995).

It's been eight years since the first charm fabric exchanges and the groups are still together. They challenge each other with new charm exchanges, round robins and block exchanges. Every year new groups sprout, including quilt-basting, doll-making, wearable art, and quilts for chronically ill children. Whether working with a theme or just working on their own projects, all the groups provide friendship, learning, advice, inspiration and a rich supportive environment where quilters can stretch their creative wings. As guilds grow, these small groups become a vital part of the quiltmaking experience.

Our first charm group had eleven members, six of whom appear in this book. At our first monthly meeting we agreed on a goal (to collect 1000 different 4″ x 4″ squares of fabric) and a set of procedures. What follows are not the procedures we used but an updated set of guidelines.

Originally we were very picky about what we would and would not accept. Small prints, stripes and plaids were requested, as were 100% cotton fabrics. Christmas prints, solids, large prints and novelties (children's prints, animals, people, etc.) were discouraged. Now that the quilts are complete, all the quilters wish they had more of the novelty prints that we snubbed in our first exchange. In a charm quilt, it is often the funny or ugly prints that attract attention and recall the fondest memories.

CHARM EXCHANGE GUIDELINES

1. Use only 100% cotton fabrics, pre-washed and pressed. Cut accurately and make sure to discard the selvage edges. Accuracy is welcome because there's always someone in the swap who wants to use the squares just as they receive them and not cut them into another shape.

2. Consider having the number of members in the group a multiple of eight. This works well because from one 5″ strip of fabric you can cut 8 squares, 5″ x 5″. Sixteen is also a good number because you can cut the squares from 3/8 yard of fabric, and you can fit sixteen people in most homes. If there are sixteen in the group, you will receive 160 different fabrics in each color exchange.

3. Assign and exchange three color groups per month. At the end of four months each person in a group of sixteen will have about 1900 fabrics (in a group of eight each will have approximately 950). Keep the color groups separate. Starting with Color Group 1, each member selects ten different fabrics from this group. Cut 5″ x 5″ swatches from each of these fabrics (one for each member of the group including yourself). Make identical stacks containing one of each of the ten different fabrics. Place the stacks in small plastic bags for each group member. If you can't attend a meeting, make sure the hostess has your bags of fabric squares before the meeting.

Color Groups
1. Reds, burgundies
2. Pinks, mauves
3. Purples, lavenders
4. Blues, teals

5. Yellows, golds

6. Oranges, rusts, browns

7. Greens, olives, aquas

8. Taupes, beiges, off-whites, whites

9. Blacks, grays

10. White background prints

11. Multi-color prints

12. Novelties, including holidays, foods, etc.

4. During the meeting, lay out all the fabrics brought by each member from each color group and have the whole group search for duplicates. There will be surprisingly few.

5. Use fabrics from your own collection, or buy new fabrics. Make sure they are pre-washed and pressed before cutting. Use the golden rule when choosing fabrics for the exchange: give fabrics that you would like to receive. Don't use this as a dumping ground for fabrics you hate and would never use!

6. Be a good guest. Debra Mellentine sacrifices her diets to partake in the delicious desserts made by the hostess! Claire Vlasin, currently the hostess of *Charming Offspring*, was especially appreciative when the other group members gave her stamps to help with correspondence. Be gracious about what you receive from others. Quite often the fabric you never thought you could use is just the fabric you need later in the quilt-making process.

7. *MOST IMPORTANT RULE:* Bring snacks! After all, fabric exchanges and searching for duplicates can be tough work, and we need to keep up our strength.

COMPUTER AND MAIL EXCHANGES

I love getting mail. I remember as a young girl waiting everyday for the mailman, hoping I'd get something, anything! I still look forward to the mail each day, only now I have something really fun to look forward to...FABRIC!!!

I've joined fabric swaps through magazines, swapping newsletters and the computer. Almost every day I can look forward to an envelope containing anywhere from seven to ten charm fabrics. These envelopes are known as "soft mail" because the envelopes feel cushy when you take them out of the mailbox. Often I receive a nice note, recipe or pattern along with the fabrics. I've received fabrics from Alabama, Alaska, Arizona, Arkansas, California, Colorado, Connecticut, Florida, Georgia, Idaho, Illinois, Indiana, Iowa, Kansas, Louisiana, Maryland, Massachusetts, Michigan, Minnesota, Mississippi, Missouri, Nebraska, Nevada, New Hampshire, New Jersey, New York, Oklahoma, Oregon, Pennsylvania, Tennessee, Texas, Utah, Virginia, Washington, West Virginia, Wisconsin, Canada and Iceland!

If you are isolated and live far from a quilt shop, or are not a member of a guild, you can exchange fabrics through the mail. In *Quilter's Newsletter Magazine*, there is a Quilters' Exchange page displaying four or five names of people who are looking for charm fabrics. If you write to these quilters and send them what they request, they will return to you in kind.

There are also newsletters devoted solely to fabric exchanges by mail. *Quilters Request Newsletter* and *Trader's Resource* are subscription newsletters that link quilters who want to trade. For a yearly subscription fee, you receive the names and addresses of quilters who are interested in many types of exchanges. Not only do they trade charm squares, they also trade quilt blocks and organize round robins. *The Charm Connection Fabric Trading Clubs* trade fabrics with a monthly theme, no subscription fee and a minimum handling fee. (See RESOURCES to contact these groups.)

Many quilting catalogs and mail order fabric companies have clubs or swatch samples for ordering. Each club is different, but they all have a set fee and send samples of the latest fabrics from different groupings, usually four times a year. Some also include a newsletter and tips; all include ways to order yardage from their samples.

Swatch samples are a one-time order and, for a fee, you receive fabric samples cut in large sizes, ranging from 3″ x 3″ to 6″ x 6″. The best place to find them is in advertisements in your favorite quilt magazines.

Computer swaps are fun and reap big fabric rewards. I subscribe to Prodigy® and swap fabrics with a group on-line. If you are new to computers, it can be a challenge to find your way around. To locate quilters on Prodigy, go to the *Crafts 2 Bulletin Board* and choose *Quilting.* You will find a wide array of topics to read and comment about. Topics that begin with *SW* are swaps. If the topic is followed by *Open,* they are looking for new members; if it is followed by *CL*, it is closed for the current exchange. There are about forty different swaps at any given time.

To participate, read the topics until you find one that is inviting new members. You can also ask existing swaps if they accept new members, or even start a swap of your own. There will be a hostess for the swap. In my swap, the hostess had us send our "snail mail" (U.S. Post Office) address through e-mail, a service provided by Prodigy and most other on-line services. She then sent out seven 5″ x 5″ charm squares to each of us, along with the addresses of twenty-three other ladies to swap with. We then sent out seven 5″ x 5″ charm squares to the names on the list. Seven charm squares and a short note fit nicely in a legal-sized envelope and take one first class stamp to mail.

Quilters are also present on America On-Line® and on the World Wide Web. Try entering *Quilts* or *Crafts* through the search feature on your on-line service to hunt for quilters.

Don't forget your local quilt shop! Many sell charm quilt fabric packets. Usually you can buy packets of 100 charm squares that are pre-cut.

Remember to look in your own fabric stash. Cut 5″ x 5″ squares of your favorite fabrics, and then add those that you purchased a long time ago and now wonder why you ever bought them! This is the perfect opportunity to use them in a project; you'll be amazed at how well they work and how much fun they are to use. Many quilters like to use their charm quilts as historical records of their fabric collections. Some even cut a charm square from every fabric they buy after it is pre-washed.

For my next charm quilt I plan to cut a square from all my fabrics to incorporate in my quilt. It's a great way to assess the strengths and weaknesses of your fabric palette. Quilts made from our own collections provide a history of modern fabric trends. Someday our daughters, granddaughters and great-granddaughters will share the same fascination with antique quilts that we enjoy today.

CHARM GAMES FOR GROUPS

I produce a quilt retreat called the *Northern Michigan Quilters Getaway.* In the supply list for the *Getaway,* I ask participants (usually about fifty quilters) to bring fifty 5″ x 5″ charm squares of one fabric, placed in zip-lock bags with their names on them. I sort the squares into fifty stacks of fifty different fabrics and return them to the bags. Everyone receives a memento of the retreat. The process of sorting takes a few hours, so if you're the organizer, schedule this time or find a helper.

Our quilt guild has charm grab bags for Christmas. Members bring ten different charm squares in brown paper bags with their names on them. They place the bags on a table and then each person selects a bag brought by someone else. We limit it to three bags per person. The beauty of this game is that it doesn't require full participation or prior knowledge of the number who plan to participate. The idea works no matter how many people join in the fun.

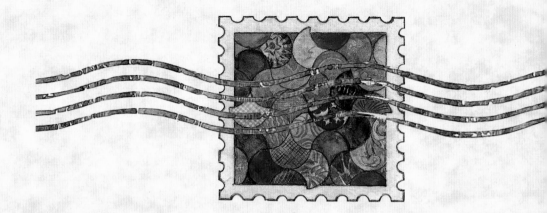

Part Two

DIRECTIONS
FOR MAKING
CHARM QUILTS

T O HELP YOU GET STARTED, I have provided a Charm Chart (page 18). This guide shows the number of different pieces you need to cut, using the templates provided. Sizes vary because the templates vary. The sizes are based on inches and standard bed sizes. Use the chart as an approximation for gathering your charm squares, not as the actual number you will use in your quilt. The chart also assumes you are not adding borders to the quilt. Borderless quilts take many more pieces than those with borders. If you want a large-size quilt, but don't want a large number of pieces, consider adding a border around all four sides, which can cut the number of pieces by twenty percent or more.

After you've acquired a great collection of charm squares, it's time to start your quilt. Before cutting into your charm fabrics, you need to choose your project.

Charm quilts have a life of their own. Trying to plan the entire quilt before sewing and cutting is frustrating. I am an organized, planning kind of quilter. I had to let go of my inhibitions and take a leap of faith to get started. Review the quilts on the following pages and read the insights from the quilters who made them. They provide valuable information about the degree of difficulty in sewing the pattern as well as laying out the colors.

Some patterns are suitable for all fabrics and have a more random feeling (Tumbler, page 43, Pyramid, page 54, Diamond, page 70). Some quilts are arranged by values of darks and lights (Braid, page 39), and some work best with darks, mediums and lights (Half-Hexagon, page 74). Other quilts are arranged by colors (Square, page 32, Honeycomb, page 82) and some quilts are sorted by units and colors (Square, page 36, Triangle, page 46 and 50, Kite, page 78, Pyramid, page 58 and Clamshell, page 96). Many quilts are inspired by quilters' fabric collections (House, page 60, Clamshell, page 91 and Apple Core page 87).

Take your time before cutting the shapes. Make a small sample of a portion of the quilt before you cut all the squares. What a shame to cut 1000 honeycombs and find you hate to set-in piece!

I made samples of each quilt in the book. My instructions include piecing order, pressing, quilting suggestions and insights into the construction process. I used three different techniques to make the samples: straight-line piecing, set-in piecing and curved piecing. The following instructions for cutting, piecing and finishing are for all the quilts. Refer to this section while working on the individual projects.

Charm Chart

	SQUARE	TRIANGLE	BRAID	TUMBLER	PYRAMID	HOUSE	DIAMOND
SMALL WALL 36″ X 36″	150	300	400	300	250	300	250
CRIB 30″ X 60″	200	400	550	300	350	300	300
LARGE WALL 51″ X 51″	300	600	800	400	500	400	450
LAP 63″ X 72″	550	1100	1500	750	950	750	850
TWIN 63″ X 87″	650	1300	1800	900	1100	900	1000
FULL 78″ X 87″	800	1600	2200	1100	1400	1100	1200
QUEEN 84″ X 93″	900	1800	2400	1200	1500	1200	1400
KING 93″ X 102″	1100	2200	3000	1500	1900	1500	1700

HEXAGON	HONEYCOMB	HALF-HEXAGON	KITE	APPLE CORE	CLAMSHELL
150	180	270	250	150	180
200	225	350	300	200	200
300	350	550	450	300	350
500	650	1000	850	550	650
600	750	1150	1000	650	750
700	900	1400	1200	800	900
800	1000	1600	1350	900	1000
1000	1250	2000	1650	1100	1250

CUTTING

Cutting the charm shapes is an important part of the quiltmaking process and the first step in guaranteeing a flat, accurate quilt top with beautifully formed intersections, points and curves.

1. Use a sharp pencil to accurately trace the templates onto see-through template plastic. Be sure to include the seam lines.

2. Use sharp scissors or rotary cutting blades for cutting fabric. Don't use your good fabric scissors or rotary blades for cutting templates.

3. Layer no more than four to six charm squares to minimize slipping.

4. Grain lines are included on the templates and are appropriate for the quilt shown. These charm shapes can be used in many ways to create different visual effects. A different placement for the charm shapes may require a different grain line alignment. Most of the charm shapes have bias edges, so be very gentle when you handle the fabrics.

5. For special fabrics that have a particular motif you want to center, make sure that the motif is on the top of the stack, or cut it alone. Center the motif inside the seam line, not the cutting line, to know exactly where the motif will end up after sewing.

6. If you are cutting with scissors, trace around the plastic template onto one charm square, layer on top of three to five other charm fabrics, and cut. If fabrics slip and shift, cut through fewer layers.

7. If you are rotary cutting, trace around the plastic template onto one charm square. Layer on top of three to five other charm fabrics and place on a small rotary cutting mat. Place the straight edge of any rotary cutting ruler on the drawn lines and cut on the lines, rotating the cutting board as you go. Each charm square requires at least three cuts to achieve the desired shape. By turning the mat instead of the layered charm squares, you can minimize shifting and slipping.

NOTE: EZ Quilting by Wrights has produced a set of acrylic templates that coordinate with the designs in this book.

Use the Easy Rule™ to cut squares, kites and honeycombs; the Easy Angle™ to cut triangles, houses and braids; and the Easy Three™ to cut pyramids, hexagons, diamonds, and half-hexagons. Here are some hints.

1. Trace the template onto see-through tracing paper instead of template plastic. Tape the paper template to the cutting ruler.

2. Place the ruler near the corner of the layered charms (don't layer more than six). Make the first two cuts to even the edges that have frayed from storage or were not cut accurately to begin with.

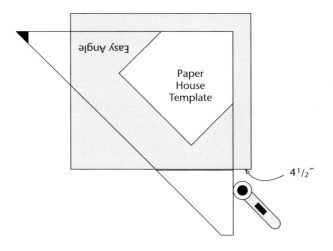

3. Rotate the board so that a justcut side aligns with at least one edge.

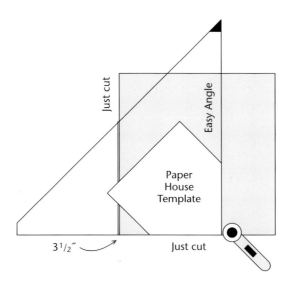

4. Continue rotating and cutting until the shape is complete.

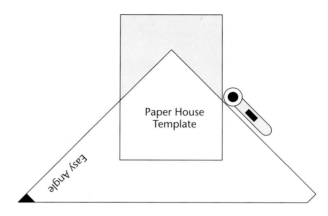

PIECING

The quilts are organized by how they are pieced, and in order of difficulty. The first set of quilts uses straight-line piecing and is great for beginners and quilters who like fast projects. The second group of quilts uses set-in piecing. This requires more starting and stopping than straight-line piecing, but produces excellent and sometimes three-dimensional results. The third set of quilts uses curved piecing or appliqué.

Straight-Line Piecing

Straight-line piecing is used for working with the Square, Braid, Tumbler, Triangle, and Pyramid charm shapes. It is a simple, straightforward technique familiar to most quilters. Here are a few tips for machine piecing. (For hand piecing, follow instructions for set-in piecing on page 23.)

1. All templates include $1/4''$ seam allowances. Maintain an accurate and consistent $1/4''$ seam while sewing pieces together.*

2. Chain-piece as you sew. When sewing the patches together, you can feed the pieces in, one pair after another, without clipping threads. This saves thread and time, and makes the sewing neater.

3. Carefully align the pieces as you sew. If two squares are to be sewn together, lay them on top of each other so that all the edges line up, not just the edges you sew. If you have cut accurately, they will line up per-

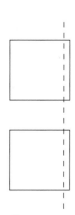

Chain piecing

fectly. If you line up only the seam you are sewing, it is easy to err slightly, causing jagged edges and mis-matched seams in future steps.

4. As the sewing progresses, you will be sewing patches into larger units. Make sure to match up edges and seams as the quilt top gets larger. Pin at seam intersections and edges to manage the longer seams as you sew.

5. Follow the pressing hints given with the quilt projects. The pressing hints are designed to make seams interlock as often as possible. When quilts are pressed properly, they lay much flatter and are easier to quilt.

6. If you choose a project that is sewn in units, first sew one unit, and then check the finished size of this unit with the finished size given in the project. If they do not correspond, adjust the seam allowance for a better fit. (If the unit comes out slightly smaller, decrease the seam allowance slightly; if the unit comes out slightly larger, increase the seam allowance slightly.)

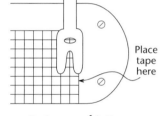

Place tape here

Finding your $^1/_4''$ seam allowance

* To find a $^1/_4''$ seam allowance, use a piece of graph paper with a $^1/_4''$ grid. Trim the paper on one of the lines; then place the paper under the presser foot. Place the needle on the $^1/_4''$ line from the edge which you trimmed. Place a piece of tape next to the edge of the paper, on the plate of the sewing machine. Do not cover the feed dogs with the tape. You now have a $^1/_4''$ seam guide to follow.

Set-In Piecing

The quilts using the House, Hexagon, Diamond, Half-Hexagon, Kite and Honeycomb charm shapes require more skill and patience. They are patterns where seams turn corners. Look at any pattern. If a line in the pattern turns a corner before reaching the edge of a piecing unit, that area requires set-in piecing. To successfully piece these shapes, you need to learn a new skill. The major change is that you start and stop each seam individually at the seam line, and not the cut edge of the fabric. For this reason many quilters prefer to do set-in seams by hand. I set-in piece just as successfully by machine as by hand. The projects can be done either way.

WARNING! Set-in piecing and hand piecing are addictive! The techniques are easy to master and the results are stunning. Often these quilts give delightful three-dimensional effects and open up a whole new world of design. The charm quilters who expressed the most joy in the actual making of their quilts were the ones who used set-in piecing by hand!

EXERCISE IN SET-IN PIECING

Let's use the diamond template to make a *Baby Block*. Try this exercise by either machine or hand.

1. After cutting three diamond charms (see CUTTING, page 20), use a C-Thru ruler® to mark the ¼″ seam line on the wrong side of each fabric. (For a three-dimensional effect, choose one light, one medium and one dark.)

2. Working with diamonds A and B, with right sides together, sew the A diamond to the B diamond on just the seam line (the pencil line you drew in Step 1). The diamonds are exactly the same size and shape. Line up all four sides of the diamonds, not just the side to be sewn. Do not sew beyond the stitching line into the seam allowance, and make sure to anchor the beginning and the end of the seam line by taking three or four backstitches.

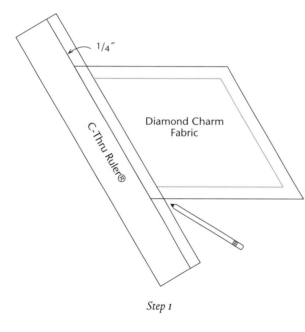

1/4″

C-Thru Ruler®

Diamond Charm
Fabric

Step 1

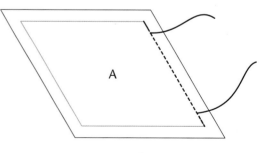

A

Step 2

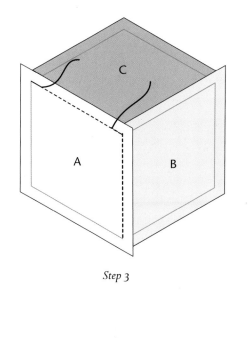

Step 3

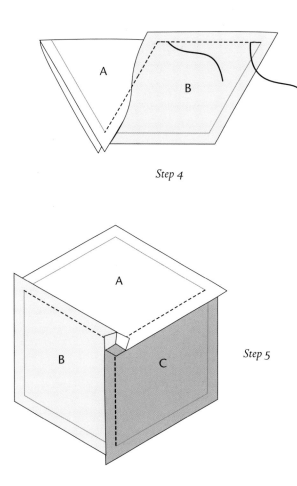

Step 4

Step 5

3. Next, with right sides together, sew the A diamond to the C diamond on just the seam line. Pull the B diamond out of the way as you line up A and C. Line up all the edges of the A and C diamonds, not just the side to be sewn. Do not sew beyond the seam line into the seam allowance, and do not sew the seam allowance from the AB seam into the current seam. Anchor the beginning and the end of the seam line by backstitching three or four stitches.

4. With right sides together, sew the B diamond to the C diamond on just the seam line. Pull the A diamond out of the way as you line up B and C. Line up all the edges of the B and C diamonds, not just the side to be sewn. Do not sew beyond the seam line into the seam allowance. Do not sew the seam allowances from the AB or the AC seams into the current seam. Make sure to anchor the beginning and the end of the seam line by taking three or four backstitches.

5. The *Baby Block* unit is now done. Press the seams in a clockwise or counter-clockwise direction, opening the set-in seam intersection as shown. Trim threads.

There are many different shapes that require set-in piecing. Apply the techniques learned with the *Baby Blocks* (page 24) anytime you need to set in a seam.

Here are some rules for set-in piecing that work for any shape.

1. Never sew into a seam allowance. Sew only from seam line to seam line. The seam allowance must remain free of stitching to allow for pivoting.

2. Never sew a seam allowance into the current seam. This inhibits pivoting in future steps. (In straight-line piecing, sew the seam from cutting line to cutting line, and press the seam in one direction. When that seam is sewn into another unit, it is sewn down.)

3. Set-in seams require more than two pieces to meet at a given point. Concentrate on only two of the fabrics at one time. Pull any other fabrics out of the way as you sew the two pieces together.

4. You can mix and match set-in piecing with straight-line piecing. In many of the following quilts a combination of set-in piecing and straight-line piecing makes the piecing fast and accurate.

5. With set-in piecing, the order of piecing is sometimes random. Many seams become zig-zagged and turn corners at funny angles. Although not orderly, these angles provide depth and movement and are well worth the effort of set-in piecing.

CURVED PIECING

The Apple Core and Clamshell charm shapes require curved piecing. Here are some hints to help you.

1. Make two templates for each charm shape, one with seam allowances and one without. Make sure to transfer the half-way lines onto the templates. These will come in handy to line up the pieces.

2. Cut out the charm shapes from the templates with seam allowances. Using a template without seam allowances, accurately center the template on the wrong side of the charm shape and transfer the sewing lines and half-way lines to the wrong side of the fabric.

3. Clip the inner curves about 3/16". Do not clip the outer curves.

4. Keep the inner curve on the top while piecing. Use the half-way marks to help line up the curves. While matching up the raw edges, the inner curve appears to have more fabric than the outer curve. Keeping the inner curve on top allows you to ease the fabric evenly and avoid tucks. The inner curve fabric likes to pull away from the outer curve, so pin generously (especially if machine piecing) and realign the raw edges as you sew.

5. This can be sewn by either hand or machine, but most quilters I know prefer to hand-piece curves.

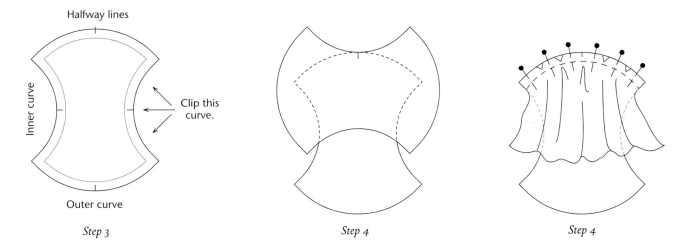

Halfway lines

Inner curve

Clip this curve.

Outer curve

Step 3   *Step 4*   *Step 4*

QUILTING

1. Cut and piece a backing fabric at least 2″ larger than the quilt top on all four sides.

2. You may pre-wash the batting (follow manufacturer's instructions) or take it out of the package and unroll it for a day beforehand to release packaging wrinkles.

3. Cut the batting the same size as the backing. I like batting with a high cotton content (at least 80%) because these batts machine quilt beautifully, don't beard and last longer.

4. Tape the backing wrong side up to a floor or table, or use a quilt frame to smooth the backing and make it as taut and wrinkle-free as possible. Lay the batting on the backing fabric and smooth.

5. Press the top for the final time and lay on top of the batting. Working from the center out, baste with safety pins or thread.

6. Machine or hand quilt, using the quilting suggestions given or choose your own pattern.

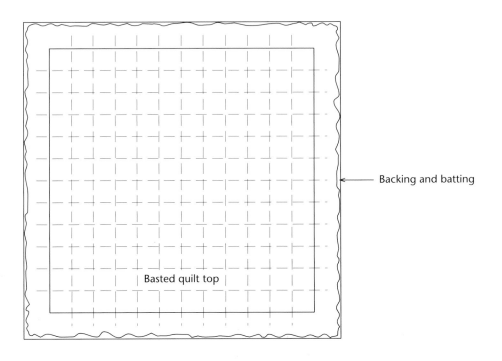

Backing and batting

Basted quilt top

BINDING

There are many different ways to finish a quilt, and binding is just one of them. There are also many different types of binding. I like to use single thickness, straight-grain binding. It is economical, easy to make, and can bind any quilt that has straight edges.

Making the Binding

1. To calculate the amount of binding you need, measure the lengths of all four sides of the quilt. The total of the four sides plus ten inches will give you the length of binding needed.

2. The binding is made from strips cut $1^1/2$″ wide. The strips are cut on the crosswise grain of fabric, so each strip is at least 40″ long. Divide the total length of binding by 40″ to obtain the number of strips needed.

3. Cut the fabric into $1^1/2$″ strips. Cut off any selvage edges (perpendicular to the length) and sew the strips together, end to end, until all strips have been joined.

4. Fold and press a generous $1/4$″ for the entire length of one side of the binding.

Applying the Binding

1. Hand or machine baste the edges of the quilt top to the batting and backing. Trim the quilt batting and backing even with the quilt top.

2. Start near the center of any side of the quilt. With right sides together, lay the binding on the quilt so the raw edge of the binding is even with the raw edge of the quilt.

3. At the starting edge of the binding, finger press the short end about $1/4$″ to the wrong side. This will finish off the binding edge when you are done with the quilt.

4. Machine-stitch the binding with a generous $1/4$″ seam allowance. (You may make minor adjustments with the seam allowance to accommodate different thicknesses of batting.)

5. Do not stitch to the end of the side. When you come to within $5/16$″ (or your adjusted seam allowance) of the corner, stop and backstitch about four stitches, and clip the threads.

6. Take the quilt out of the machine and fold the miters. This is a two-part process. The first fold will divide the corner in half by folding it at a

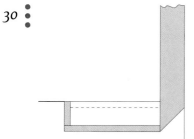

Quilt front

Step 6

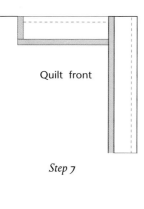

Quilt front

Step 7

45° angle. The folded edge of the binding should line up with the raw edge of the next side of the quilt.

7. The second fold brings the binding straight down. The fold itself will line up on the quilt side you have already sewn, and the raw edge of the binding will lay on top of the raw edge of the next side of the quilt.

8. Start sewing at the top fold. When you come to within 5/16″ of the edge, repeat the miter and continue until all four sides and corners are sewn.

9. Overlap the binding about 1/2″ to cover the fold where you started. Back-stitch and clip off any extra binding.

10. Hand stitch the long folded edge of the binding to the back side of the quilt. Use a blind stitch and make sure you go through only the back layer of the quilt.

11. The back corners are mitered by making two folds, the first straight across and the second straight down. As you hand stitch, it helps to blind-stitch the miters down on both the front and back of the quilt.

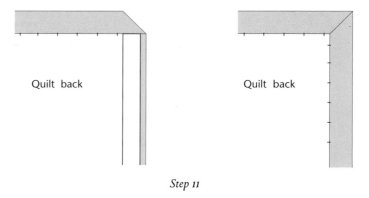

Quilt back   Quilt back

Step 11

Congratulations, your quilt is done! Make a cup of tea or coffee, lay out your quilt and admire your work. If you're like me, you will allow yourself only five minutes, since you're already planning your next charm quilt!

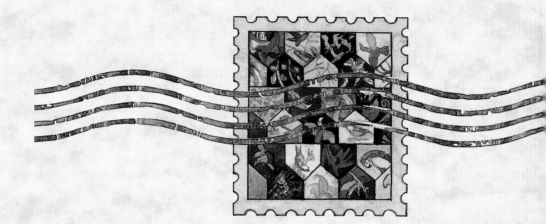

Part Three

PROJECTS

A Charming Trip Around the Capitol City Quilt Guild

LANSING, MICHIGAN, 1991

483 SQUARES, 78 X 92 INCHES

MACHINE PIECED AND HAND QUILTED

 AISY'S QUILT is the perfect place to start our study of charm quilts. She used the simplest shape in a traditional *Trip Around the World* setting for this wonderful quilt. She has also completed many smaller projects using charm squares and is one of the keepers of the charm flame!

Daisy has sewn all her life and saved fabric scraps for more than fifty years. When her daughter left for college in 1979, Daisy turned her sewing skills to quiltmaking. Some fabrics in this quilt were from dresses sewn for herself and her daughter, and bring back many memories. In 1986 a diagnosis of cancer became a turning point, and during her successful recovery she dedicated herself to quiltmaking. Daisy enjoys hostessing the original charm exchange group and the *Daughters of Charm* each month for a potluck supper.

Originally Daisy had planned to make a *Thousand Pyramids* quilt. She laid out all the patches on a sheet placed on the bed in her spare room. After rearranging them by color, she began to see the *Trip Around the World* setting and decided to use the Square shape. The quilt was laid out with that setting in mind. Daisy found that more than just the fabrics from the fabric exchange were needed to complete the pattern, so she chose from her own stash to finish the top.

After all the pieces were laid out, Daisy began the sewing process. The quilt was pieced on the machine in nine-patch units. She carried one nine-patch at a time from the bed, sewed it, pressed it, then returned it to its position on the bed. This way the order of the layout was maintained. The nine-patches were sewn into rows and the rows sewn together. Daisy included a center block based on the Capitol City Quilt Guild logo, and added two borders to complete the top.

The top was then layered with batting and backing and hand quilted. She chose a simple quilting motif that followed the *Trip Around the World* setting and avoided many seam allowances. Most of the quilting was done in hotel rooms while Daisy accompanied her husband Clark on business trips.

DIRECTIONS FOR *A Charming Trip Around the Capitol City Quilt Guild*

Use the illustration of the 16-patch unit to guide you in the sewing and pressing of the quilt top. I found the 16-patch unit to my liking because working with an even number of blocks made the pressing simpler. The pressing is planned so all the seams meet and face in opposite directions, as explained in the diagram below.

1. After playing with the charm squares and deciding on their arrangement, carefully place a unit of 16 squares next to the machine. Sew to make four vertical rows of four squares each. Press the seams in the vertical rows as shown.

2. Pin to match the edges and seams. Sew the vertical rows together to form the 16-patch unit. In this row and all the odd numbered rows, press the seams as shown. The unit should now measure 12½″ x 12½″.

3. Continue making units to complete the first row of the quilt.

4. On even numbered rows, make the units as you did in Step 1. When you press the vertical seams from Step 2, press them in the opposite direction. This will help the quilt top lay flat when you sew the rows together.

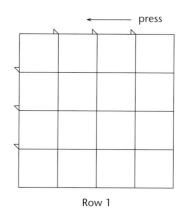

Row 1

Step 2

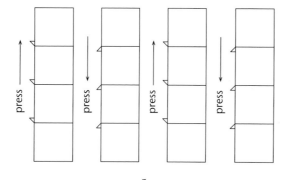

Step 1

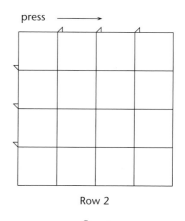

Row 2

Step 4

The simple straight line quilting motif follows the darks and lights of the *Trip* *Around the World* setting. This quilting design is suitable for both hand and machine quilting.

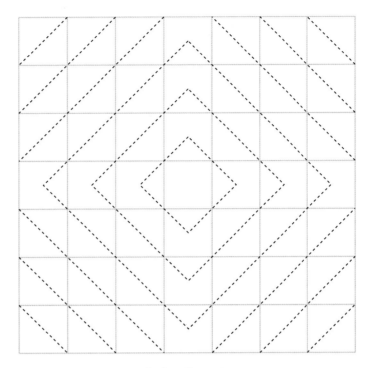

Quilting Suggestion

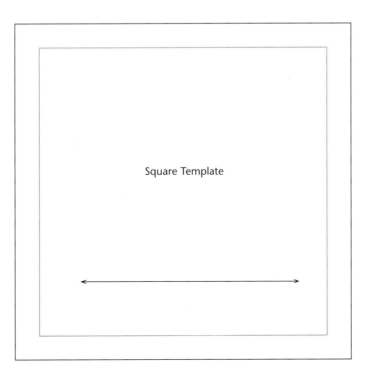

Square Template

Tropical C's

MARY ELLEN, who lives in Key Largo, Florida, has been sewing since she was nine years old. She started making Barbie doll clothes and then graduated to her own clothing. Even at the age of nine her work was beautiful. She won a blue ribbon in a contest for a hostess apron. It was exciting for me, because she's my sister! I remember her sitting in the basement, sewing on our mother's old black Singer straight-stitch machine. While Mary Ellen completed beautiful garment after garment, I produced an entire line of unfinished, badly sewn clothes.

As we grew and carved out our separate lives, Mary Ellen's creative skills led to more sewing and a successful business producing one-of-a-kind baby blankets. I dabbled in many fiber crafts and found my way to quiltmaking. In 1988, after quilting for six years, I was finally ready to introduce my sister to this wonderful sewing expression. She thought I was nuts to cut up fabric, only to sew it together for bedspreads! However, I knew that with her excellent sewing skills and quick mind, quilting would be right up her alley. Together we began a king-sized *Jacob's Ladder* bed quilt. It took us two weeks to make the top, and from that moment on she became an avid quilter and fabric collector. She loves to attend shows, workshops and group meetings, and tries not to leave any fabric store unshopped. Mary Ellen enjoys the camaraderie of quiltmaking, and we both agree that our shared interest in quilting has brought us closer together.

Mary Ellen made *Tropical C's* specifically for this book. I knew that the south Florida lifestyle had given her a taste for bright tropical fabrics and I wanted to include another quilt made from the Square charm shape. She collected the fabrics through three exchanges, one with Florida friends, one with Prodigy quilters, and one by mail with quilters in Ohio.

The quilt is machine pieced and machine quilted, using a clamshell design. The entire quilt took one week to make! The layout was inspired by a drawing in *Introduction to Tesselations* by Jill Britton and Dale Seymour. Two hundred and forty charm squares were pieced for the center of the quilt. A 3″ (3½″ cut) purple inner border separates seventy-six additional charm squares and then the purple fabric repeats in a 5″ border, creating a simple to piece but very effective marquee frame.

DIRECTIONS FOR *Tropical C's*

1. Use a design wall to arrange the squares, 12 across by 20 down, to form interlocking C shapes. Each C is made from five squares. Sort the charm squares into stacks of five that are close in color, value and pattern scale. To make the C's stand out, place them next to very different C's. For example, a pink C will stand out from a blue C more than a blue C will stand out from a green C.

2. For sewing and pressing, follow the same instructions for *A Trip Around the Capitol City Quilt Guild* quilt (page 34).

3. Cut two strips of purple fabric, 3½″ x 60½″, and sew to the long sides of the quilt. Press toward the purple fabric. Cut two strips of purple fabric, 3½″ x 42½″, and sew to the top and bottom of the quilt. Press toward the purple fabric.

4. Sew twenty-two charm squares end-to-end to form a strip. Press the seams to one side, then sew to one long side of the quilt. Repeat the charm strip and sew to the opposite side of the quilt. Press toward the purple fabric.

5. Sew sixteen charm squares end-to-end to form a strip. Press the seams to one side, then sew to the top of the quilt. Repeat the procedure and sew the strip to the bottom of the quilt. Press the seams toward the purple fabric.

6. Cut two strips of purple fabric, 5½″ x 72½″, and sew to the long sides of the quilt. Press toward the purple fabric. Cut two strips of purple fabric, 5½″ x 58½″, and sew to the top and bottom of the quilt. Press toward the purple fabric.

7. Machine quilt, using the clamshell template as a pattern (page 95).

Step 1

Fourth of July

*by Norine Antuck and
Beth Donaldson*

LANSING, MICHIGAN, 1996

452 BRAIDS, 39 X 39 INCHES

MACHINE PIECED AND MACHINE QUILTED

I T WAS FUN to make a quilt with my friend Norine, a retired registered nurse who began quilting in 1980. She has made numerous bed, wall and crib quilts. She spends about three days each week attending local quilt-related activities, and her needle skills have expanded to include doll-making, needlepoint and cross-stitch.

Norine was working with the Braid shape set in a square unit. When the squares were put together, stars appeared. After seeing Norine's version, I was intrigued by the setting and played with the braid and its mirror image. I came up with a new version that tesselates and reminds me of fireworks. The braid template is small enough to cut from a four-inch square, and is perfect for wall hangings.

When the design was complete, I asked for Norine's help to piece the quilt top. She's known throughout the guild for fast and accurate machine production and, when a deadline approached, she was my life-saver. The fabrics came from my collection and from exchanges Norine made through Prodigy, e-mail and with the *Charming Offspring* group.

DIRECTIONS FOR *Fourth of July*

1. Making the fireworks and tesselations stand out requires four different colors. Red, white, tan and navy carry out a patriotic theme. For each unit, choose one white, one red, two navy and two tan braids.

2. Trace the cutting line of the template on the wrong side of the white braid. Notice the cut-off tips on the braid template. These are cut off to make lining up the tricky 45° angle a breeze while sewing.

3. The braid is a shape that has a mirror image. Both the braid and its mirror image are used in each block. Layer the six charms from Step 1 in this order: one tan right side up, one tan wrong side up, one navy right side up, one navy wrong side up, one red wrong side up, and the white braid from Step 2, wrong side up. Cut on the traced line through all the fabrics.

4. Sew the braids together to make three strips. Press as shown.

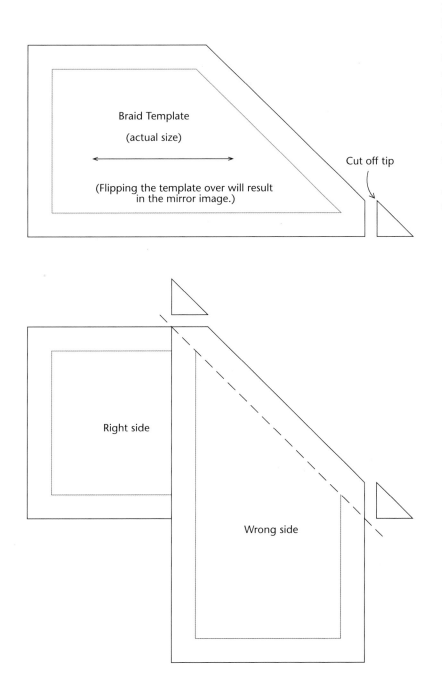

Braid Template

(actual size)

(Flipping the template over will result in the mirror image.)

Cut off tip

Right side

Wrong side

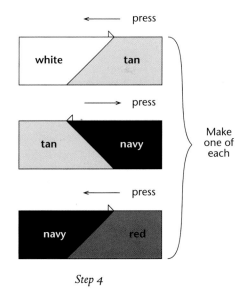

press

white   tan

press

tan   navy

press

navy   red

Make one of each

Step 4

5. Sew three strips together as shown to make one square, 5″ x 5″. Press away from the center strip. Continue making units.

6. To sew the units into rows, rotate every other unit and press the seams all in one direction. On the next row, press the seams in the opposite direction. After two rows are sewn together, stars begin to appear and tessellate!

7. Norine's quilt is 8 units across and 8 units down. She added a border strip of red braids to complete the piece.

8. It was then layered with batting and backing, and free motion machine-quilted. The red and white charms were quilted in crescents, the navy charms in a loopy design and the tan charms were stippled.

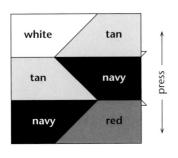

Step 5

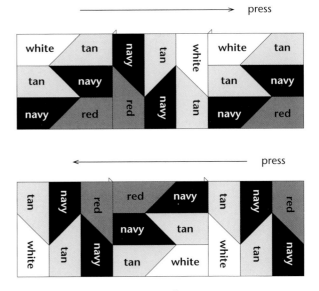

Step 6

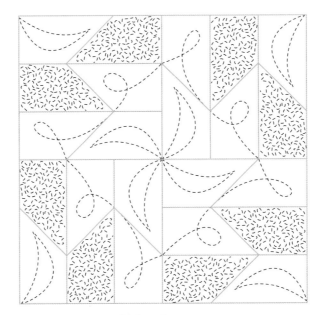

Quilting Suggestion

Tumblers on Parade

by Ruth Farmer

LANSING, MICHIGAN, 1991
696 TUMBLERS, 83 X 83 INCHES
MACHINE PIECED AND MACHINE QUILTED BY THE
HEARTS ALL AROUND QUILT SHOP,
JACKSON, MICHIGAN

RUTH IS A WOMAN of many accomplishments, with an MA in Adult Continuing Education, Women's Studies and Human Ecology. She taught vocational Home Economics until her retirement. In addition to quiltmaking, she makes time for her two children, two grandchildren and volunteering on church and advisory committees, including Community Mental Health and the Ingham County Children's Trust Fund.

Although Ruth has extensive sewing experience, this is her first quilt! While on an Elderhostel quilting vacation in Iowa, she chose the Tumbler for her pattern shape. She inquired in a quilt shop about charm quilts and the experienced quilters there told her the tumbler would be an easy quilt for a beginner.

To make her quilt look old-fashioned, Ruth used a random color layout. She sewed the tumblers together in rows of twenty-nine. After making twenty-four rows, she arranged them and sewed them together to form the top. This gives the quilt a totally scrappy feel.

After the rows were pieced, the quilt top was left with uneven edges on the sides. Ruth sought advice from other group members. Georgia Hayden suggested trimming the edges to make them straight, and attaching a striped border. Ruth took her up on both ideas, trimming the side edges, and adding two borders. She then layered it with batting and backing and had it professionally machine quilted with a heart motif.

DIRECTIONS FOR *Tumblers on Parade*

When making a sample of this pattern, I understood why the Iowa quilters recommended the tumbler shape for beginners. It is fun, fast and easy to sew. Here are a few hints to help you along.

1. Cut off the tips of fabric as shown below. This helps line up the edges as you sew the tumblers into rows.

2. When the rows are complete, press the seams in opposite directions.

3. When the rows are sewn together, they fit well and their seam allowances interlock. The top and bottom of the quilt top are straight, but the sides are uneven. Trim the side edges even, and then add borders or prepare for quilting.

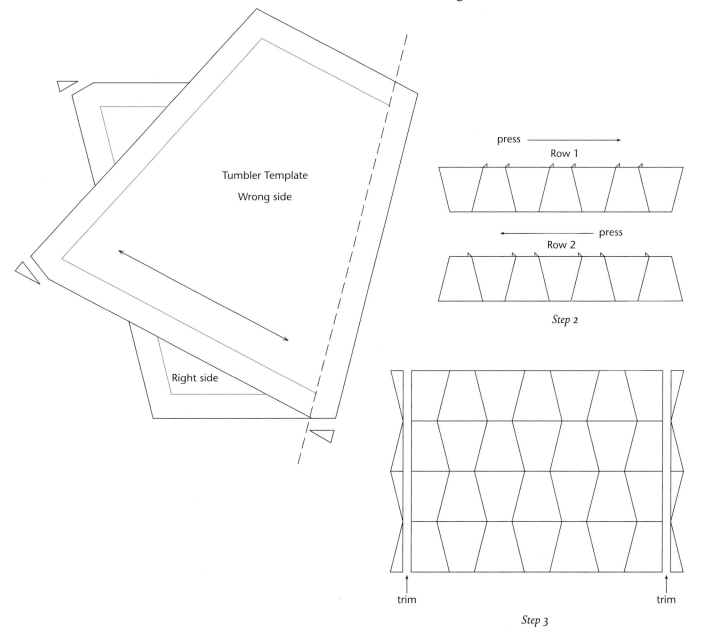

Tumbler Template

Wrong side

Right side

press ⟶

Row 1

⟵ press

Row 2

Step 2

trim   trim

Step 3

The Seven Year Itch

LANSING, MICHIGAN, 1995
1560 TRIANGLES, 78 X 90 INCHES
MACHINE PIECED AND MACHINE QUILTED

HEN I BECAME a member of the original charm group, I'd been quilting for six years and teaching for three. The charm squares from our fabric exchange simmered in my UFO pile for seven years before I resurrected them for this quilt. I chose triangles because they are easy and fast to piece, and I thought all these wonderful pieces might make a great colorwash charm quilt. After reading through and trying out some of the colorations in Deirdre Amsden's book, *Colourwash for Quilters*, I realized this was not as easy as it looked. The thought of moving 1500 triangles on a design wall was overwhelming. Further in the book I found the Marsh Quilters' *Sweet Pea Pinwheel* quilt, which suggested a way to reduce the number of pieces before moving them around on a design wall.

I sorted the triangles by colors, and then divided each color into dark, medium and light stacks. I tried to make each pinwheel either dark and light, dark and medium, or medium and light. Good contrast was needed to make sure the pinwheels showed. It was easy to keep the contrast high between darks and lights, but harder to maintain between the darks and mediums and the mediums and lights.

One of the tricks I used was to take advantage of the scale of the pattern to achieve contrast. If a dark and medium were too similar, I tried to pair a dark but busy large scale print with a medium, low contrast, small scale print. When most of the pinwheels were completed, I bribed my fifteen year old daughter Katy to arrange them on the design wall. (I'll do anything to avoid a design wall!) She came up with the ingenious giant pinwheel setting. Thank you Katy!

I planned the rest of the quilt on graph paper to count the number of pinwheels needed for each color. I also made some pinwheels that used two colors, and one that used all eight colors, to make the giant pinwheel meet in the center.

DIRECTIONS FOR *The Seven Year Itch*

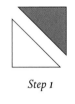

Step 1

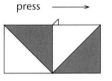

Step 3

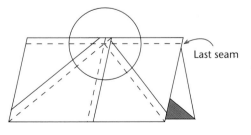

Step 4

1. To make one pinwheel, use eight triangles of the same color: four of one value, four of another. The example uses four dark and four light triangles.

2. Sew one light triangle to one dark triangle on their long sides. Press toward the dark triangle. The finished square is $3^1/_2$″ x $3^1/_2$″.

3. Sew the units into rectangles. Make sure that you sew a dark triangle next to a light triangle. Press toward the light triangle as shown.

4. Sew the rectangles together to make a square, $6^1/_2$″ x $6^1/_2$″. Working from the wrong side, pull out the stitches at the top of the last seam. This will allow you to press the seams in a circular motion. All the seams will turn in either a clockwise or counter-clockwise direction, and after pressing will lie flat as a pancake.

Last seam

Step 4

Pull out these stitches on both sides of the seam.

Step 4

5. To make the giant pinwheel setting, you need to use one pinwheel for the center that includes all the colors in the quilt, and several pinwheels that use two different colors as shown.

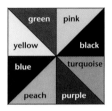

Center pinwheel with all the colors

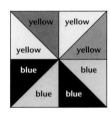

This pinwheel is an example of where two colors meet **horizontally.**

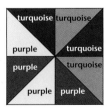

Use this pinwheel where two colors meet **diagonally.**

Step 5

6. Lay out all the pinwheels and sew into rows. As you complete the rows, press the seams in opposite directions. Then sew the rows to make the quilt top.

7. Layer the top with the batting and the backing. I machine quilted in the ditch around the pinwheels. As the colors of the giant pinwheel changed on the edges, I changed the colors of the binding to match.

press ⟶

Row 1

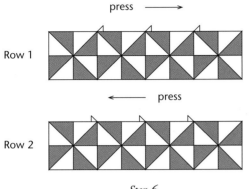

⟵ press

Row 2

Step 6

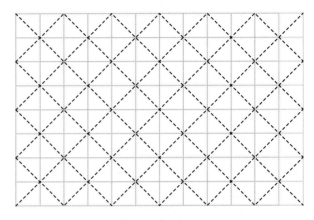

Quilting Suggestion

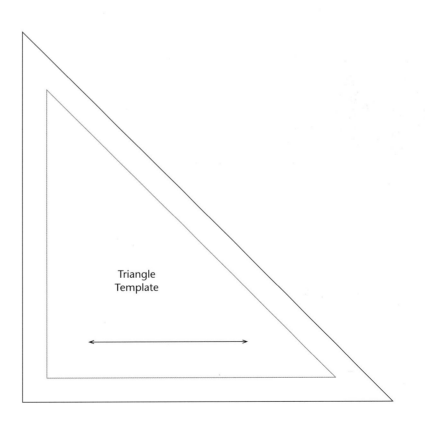

Triangle
Template

She Runs Hot and Cold

EAST LANSING, MICHIGAN, 1996

3456 TRIANGLES (1728 ON EACH SIDE), 72 X 108 INCHES

MACHINE PIECED AND MACHINE QUILTED

 F ALL THE CHARM QUILTERS who contributed to this book, Phyllis must have the best collection of charm fabrics. Not only is she a member of the first two charm exchange groups, but also she subscribes to a fabric club, and for many years she cut a four-inch square from every fabric she bought. No wonder she did a double-sided quilt! She originally joined the charm quilt group for the small group experience rather than for the charm fabrics.

Phyllis started sewing the triangles together in the units described on page 52. The wonderful placement of color values makes this quilt glow and shimmer. The first side of the quilt is based on her favorite colors, blue and green. She still had thousands of charm squares left, so she decided to make it two-sided, placing warm colors on the other side of the quilt. Phyllis found working on the quilt during the daylight hours was essential to sort out the color values.

DIRECTIONS FOR *She Runs Hot and Cold*

1. Each unit has 12 light triangles, 28 medium triangles, and 32 dark triangles from one color family, for a total of 72 triangles. The unit measures $18\frac{1}{2}''$ x $18\frac{1}{2}''$ when complete.

2. The unit is subdivided to make sewing faster. There are many places in the unit where six pieces meet. Careful pressing helps match points and keeps the work flat.

3. To make the center, choose four light and four medium triangles. Sew each light triangle to each dark triangle on their long sides to make squares $3\frac{1}{2}''$ x $3\frac{1}{2}''$. Press as shown. Sew the squares into two rectangles, pairing up the squares that were pressed in opposite directions. Sew the rectangles together to make one square, $6\frac{1}{2}''$ x $6\frac{1}{2}''$.

4. To make the sides, choose 16 dark, 8 medium and 8 light triangles. Sew each medium triangle and light triangle to a dark triangle on their long sides to make 16 squares, $3\frac{1}{2}''$ x $3\frac{1}{2}''$. Press as shown. Sew the squares into rectangles, pairing up the squares that were pressed in opposite directions and keeping the mediums and lights together. Press as shown. Sew the rectangles together to make squares $6\frac{1}{2}''$ x $6\frac{1}{2}''$ and press as shown.

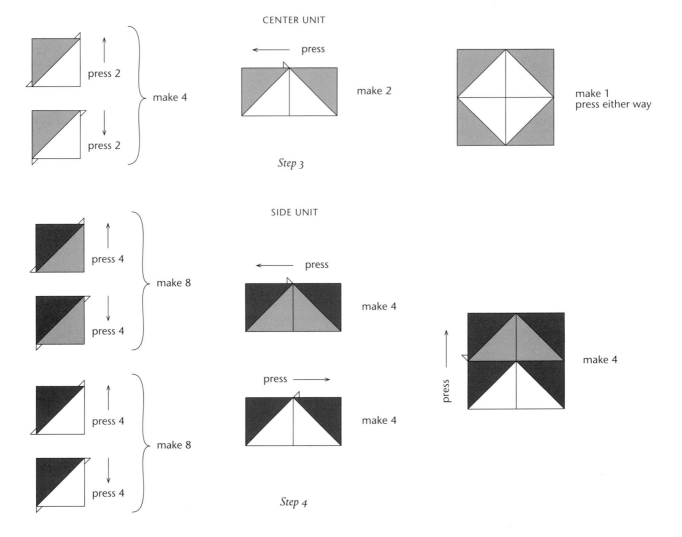

CENTER UNIT

press 2 / press 2 — make 4

← press — make 2

make 1
press either way

Step 3

SIDE UNIT

press 4 / press 4 — make 8

← press — make 4

press 4 / press 4 — make 8

press → — make 4

press — make 4

Step 4

CORNER UNIT

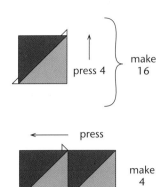

press 4

make 16

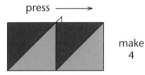

← press

make 4

press →

make 4

press

make 4

Step 5

5. To make the corners, choose 16 dark triangles and 16 medium triangles. Sew each dark triangle and medium triangle together on their long sides to make 16 squares, $3^1/_2$″ x $3^1/_2$″. Press toward the dark triangles. Sew the squares into rectangles, and press as shown. Sew the rectangles together to make squares, $6^1/_2$″ x $6^1/_2$″, pairing up the rectangles that were pressed in opposite directions. Press as shown.

6. Sew the corners, sides and center units in columns of three and press as shown. Sew the last two vertical seams and press away from the center. When you've finished sewing the units, sew them into rows and then sew the rows together to make the top.

Phyllis layered the top, batting and back, then machine quilted a free-hand curlicue in each triangle.

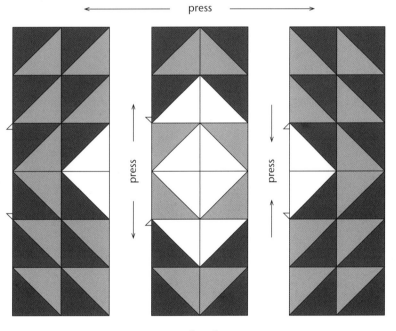

Step 6

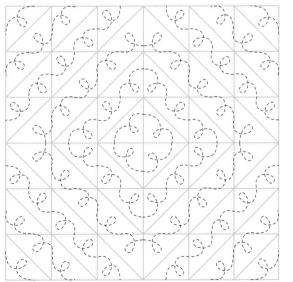

Quilting Suggestion

A Tribute to Edna and My Prince Charming

CADILLAC, MICHIGAN, 1989
1032 PYRAMIDS, 89 X 96 INCHES
MACHINE PIECED AND HAND QUILTED

F YOU'VE NEVER ventured beyond squares and right tri-angles, this Pyramid shape offers an opportunity to explore new designs in an easy-to-piece format.

This was one of Debra's first quilting projects. Her husband Tom helped choose the pattern and then made a frame to fit over the guest bed, which she used instead of a design wall. Debra took a playful approach to this fun and easy-to-use shape. She grouped the charms by color and arranged lights and darks to enhance hidden shapes in the overall design. Look for stars, baby blocks, large pyramids, hexagons and ice cream cones to pop out of the quilt.

She sewed the pyramids in a simple row-by-row format, perfect for straight-line piecing. She carried one row at a time from the upstairs bed-room to her sewing machine in the family room. While sewing the first blue rows, she accidentally mixed up the order and created new shapes on the spot. She then refined a system that kept her pieces in order as she sewed.

Debra collected most of her fabrics as a member of the Daughters of Charm group. Cindy Mielock and Phyllis O'Connor helped fill in the fabrics needed to complete the quilt top. Another important contributor to her charm stack was Edna Swisher, the mother of her husband Tom's closest friend. After Edna passed away, there was a large garage sale. Edna had such a huge collection of fabrics that even after the sale Debra became the lucky owner of multiple boxes of fabric. Many of these fab-rics were used for trading and as pieces in the quilt.

DIRECTIONS FOR *A Tribute to Edna and My Prince Charming*

1. Sew the pyramids together to make rows. When the rows are complete, press the seams in opposite directions.

2. When the rows are sewn together, they fit well and their seam allowances interlock. The top and bottom of the quilt top are straight, but the edges are uneven. Trim the side edges even, and then add borders or prepare for quilting.

QUILTING SUGGESTION

Debra outline-quilted each pyramid about 3/8″ from the edge. Traditionally, outline quilting is done 1/4″ from the edge of each piece, but Debra felt she would need to do less quilting if she increased this distance. I think it also looks better!

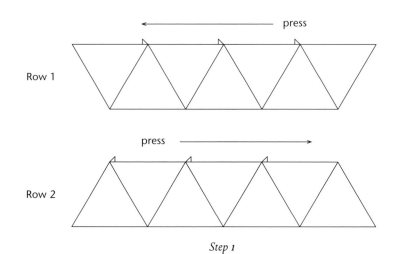

Step 1

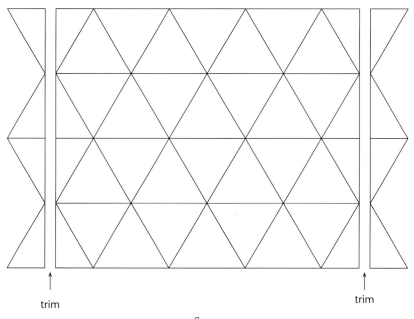

Step 2

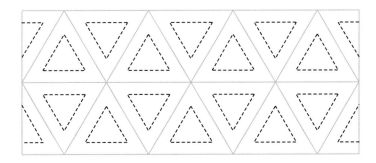

Quilting Suggestion

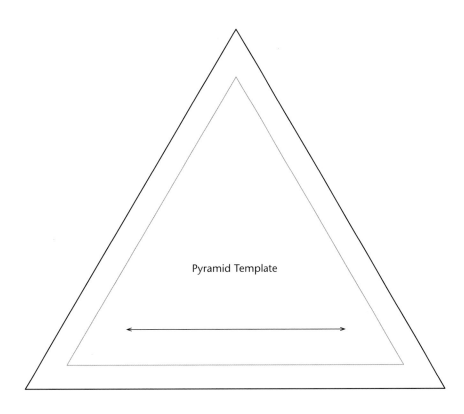

Pyramid Template

1000 Pyramids

LANSING, MICHIGAN, 1996
1664 PYRAMIDS, 75 X 72 INCHES
HAND AND MACHINE PIECED
AND MACHINE QUILTED

INDY'S LIFE-LONG LOVE of sewing turned into a passion for quiltmaking in 1980. Since then, she has been one of the most prolific quiltmakers in the area. Her range of activities includes quilt block exchanges, round robins, teaching quilt-making, winning ribbons, traveling to quilt shows, donating quilts for critically ill children, serving on the board of directors and as president of the guild, serving on quilt show committees, and hostessing a basting group that meets in her dining room. In addition to making twenty full-size quilts and more than fifty wall hangings, she also works full time.

Cindy has an extensive fabric collection that keeps growing. She's not only a contemporary quiltmaker but also a collector of fabrics for future textile historians. For the *1000 Pyramids* quilt, she challenged herself to use only fabrics from her own collection. With few exceptions, she has done this in a smashing fashion!

Cindy used the same shape as Debra Mellentine, but in a different setting. She organized her fabrics by color and then used the colors to build units. Each unit consists of sixteen pyramids, set as a larger pyramid. First she laid out the larger sixteen pyramid units on squares of a flannel backed tablecloth, which made the units portable for hand piecing (seventy-five percent of this quilt was hand pieced). After finishing several units, she placed them on a larger design wall and made additional units to blend the already finished units together. When all the units were complete, the top and bottom were straight but the sides were uneven. She chose a nondescript fabric and pieced triangles to make straight sides.

DIRECTIONS FOR *1000 Pyramids*

1. After choosing and laying out the 16 pyramids by color, sew them into rows and press as shown.

2. Sew the rows together to make one pyramid and press as shown. Careful pressing will help as you assemble the large pyramids. The base of the pyramid is 14 1/2″ and the height is 12 3/4″.

3. Refer to the diagrams on page 61 for sewing the large pyramids into large rows. Piece large triangle units for the edges as Cindy did. You may also piece 10 pyramids together to fill in the sides, and then trim the edges.

QUILTING SUGGESTION
Cindy chose simple stitch in the ditch, straight-line machine quilting. The quilting encompasses every other pyramid charm shape.

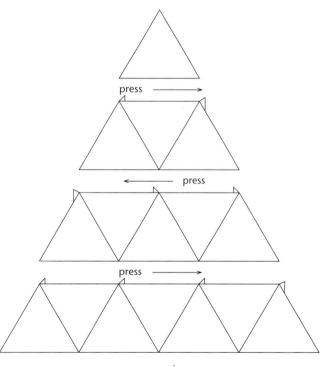

Step 1

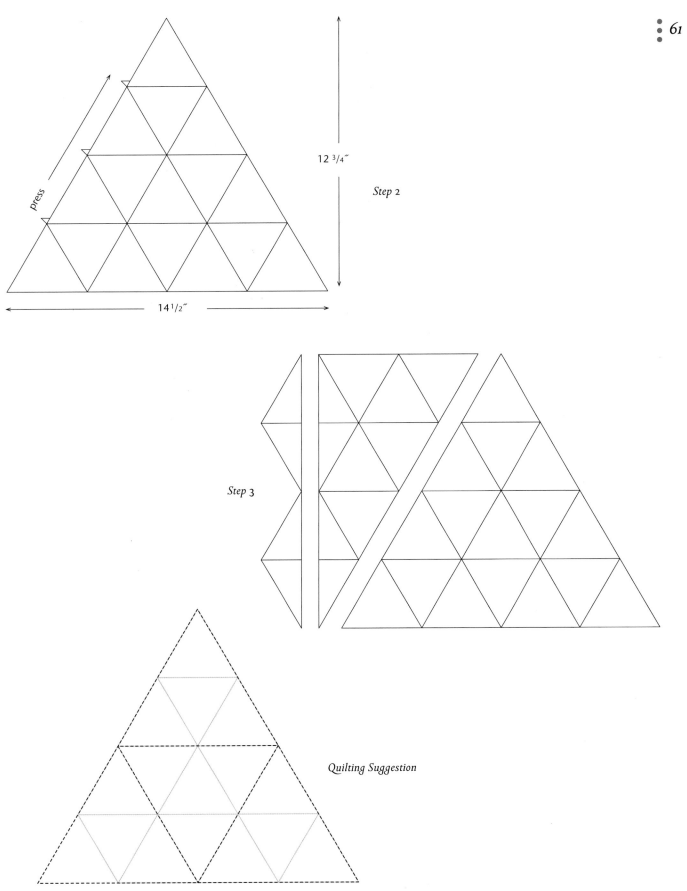

press

$12\,^3/_4''$

Step 2

$14\,^1/_2''$

Step 3

Quilting Suggestion

Birdominium

LANSING, MICHIGAN, 1996

300 HOUSES, 50^1/$_2$ X 50^1/$_2$ INCHES

HAND AND MACHINE PIECED;

MACHINE QUILTED

RUTH IS A FOUNDING MEMBER of the Capitol City Quilt Guild and our resident attorney. One of Ruth's specialties is copyright law, about which she has written a book, as well as articles for *Quilter's Newsletter Magazine.* She has always been generous with her knowledge and expertise, and all of us in the area quilting community have great respect for her.

Ruth began quilting in 1980, and a trademark of her quilts has been the inclusion of a bird fabric in many of her pieces. *Birdominium* is a showcase of her extensive collection of bird fabrics, purchased at local fabric shops and collected on road trips. Some of the fabrics are vintage 1950s; others have traveled from France and Australia to become part of her stash, and many have come from friends and relatives who surprise her with gifts of bird fabrics.

Twenty different navy or dark prints were used to fill in the edges of the rows. The rest of the quilt consists of two hundred and seventy-nine bird prints and one cat print! Ruth sorted her bird prints into darks and lights, and by sewing the houses dark-light-dark-light, etc., she created diagonal streaks running through the quilt.

DIRECTIONS FOR *Birdominium*

1. Trace and cut out the house template, including the seam allowance. On the wrong side of the fabric, draw the seam lines of the house roof.

2. Sew the sides of the houses together to form rows. Sew from the cut edge of the house base to the seam lines of the roof top. To make the diagonal design shown in Ruth's quilt, make half the rows start with a dark fabric and half the rows start with a light fabric.

3. Use set-in piecing techniques to sew the zigzag roof top seams together (pages 23–25). Press the seams in either direction after the row is sewn. Ruth sewed this seam by hand.

4. Trim the house shapes to even the sides; then sew the rows together to complete the top. The seam of one house lies in the center of another house. This seam does not need to be set in.

QUILTING SUGGESTION
Ruth machine quilted in the ditch across the rows and the zigzag seams. There is also 1/4″ outline quilting on every other dark strip.

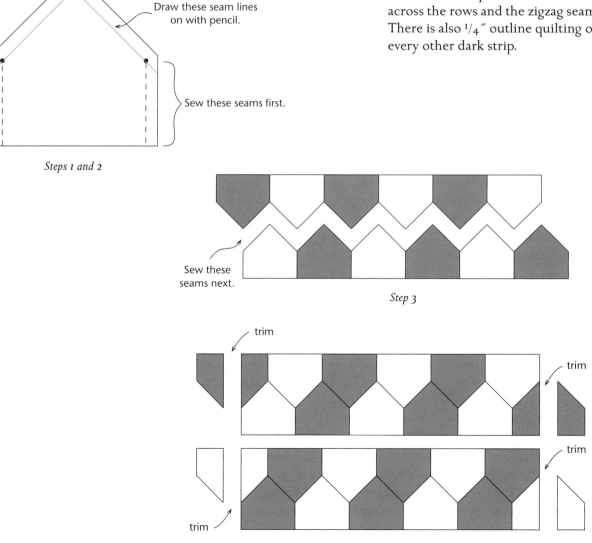

Draw these seam lines on with pencil.

Sew these seams first.

Steps 1 and 2

Sew these seams next.

Step 3

trim

trim

trim

trim

Step 4

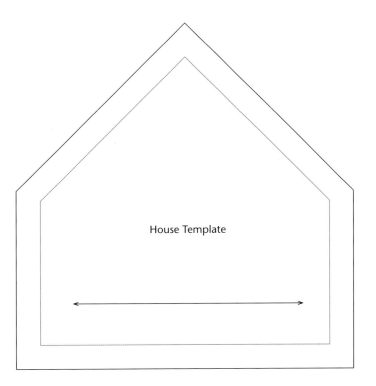

House Template

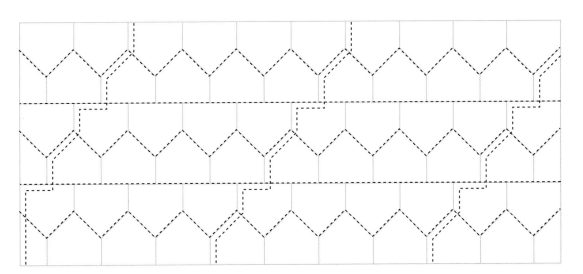

Quilting Suggestion

I've Got the Chemistry Blues

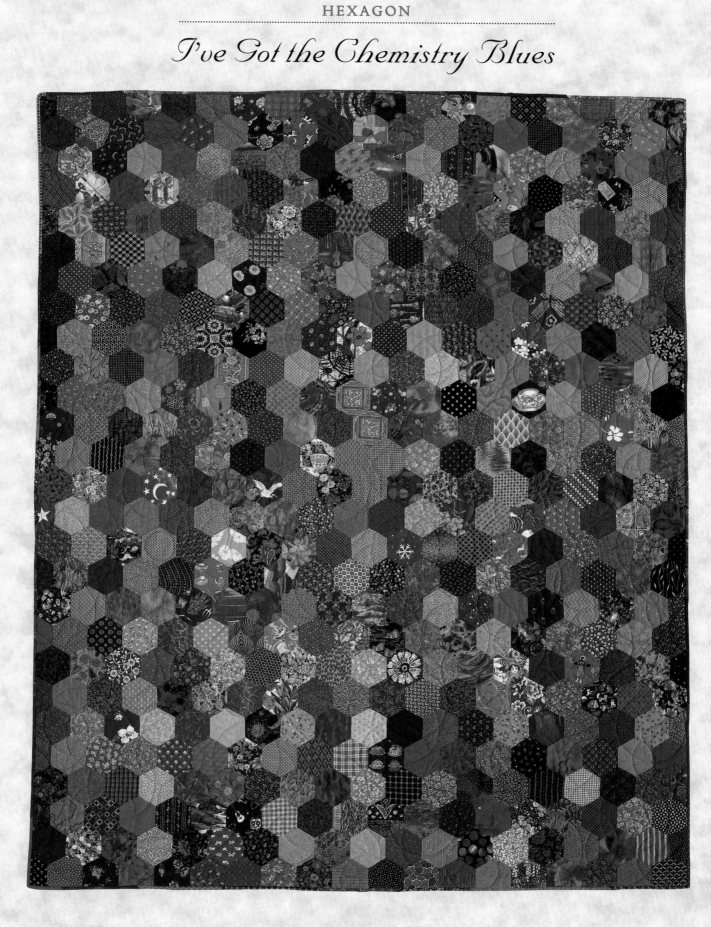

TERI NESSIA AND I share the same career. We are that rare breed of the brave, the strong and the endangered species of the Stay at Home Mom! Teri has a degree in African Studies from Michigan State University and spent her early career working in the student aid department. After the birth of her sons, she started quilting, and wrote our guild newsletter, *As the Needle Turns,* for four years.

This quilt was a gift for Teri's husband Jon on their twentieth wedding anniversary. He's a chemist, and hexagons are used liberally throughout chemistry texts as a symbol denoting chemical and molecular bonds. Her oldest son Ben is currently taking chemistry and even her younger son Nate requested a periodic table for his birthday. Teri is now spending most of her evening meals with her family discussing and memorizing periodic tables and their abbreviations, hence the title of her quilt!

The hexagon is a fascinating shape that most quilters equate with the traditional *Grandmother's Flower Garden* quilts of the 1930s. Teri chose a random setting for her dark and medium blue fabrics to produce a stunning modern quilt from this favorite shape.

DIRECTIONS FOR *I've Got the Chemistry Blues*

1. Trace and cut the templates and fabrics as described on page 20, and then follow the directions for set-in piecing on pages 23–26. After laying out the fabrics, sew the hexagons into rows. Make sure you sew only from seam allowance to seam allowance.

2. Sew the rows together with a zigzag set-in seam to complete the quilt top. This top has uneven edges. To straighten the edges, trim the top, bottom and sides of the quilt.

QUILTING SUGGESTION
Teri chose to quilt circles on the quilt top. The circles are random in size and placement. This is a great way to use your plates and saucers as quilting designs.

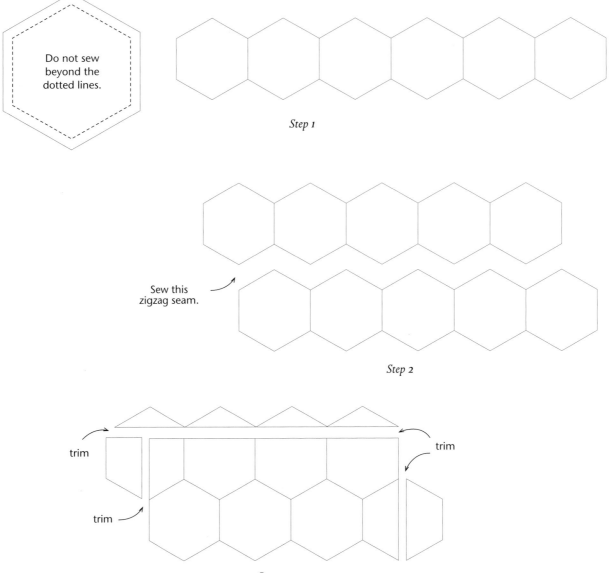

Do not sew beyond the dotted lines.

Step 1

Sew this zigzag seam.

Step 2

trim

trim

trim

trim

Step 2

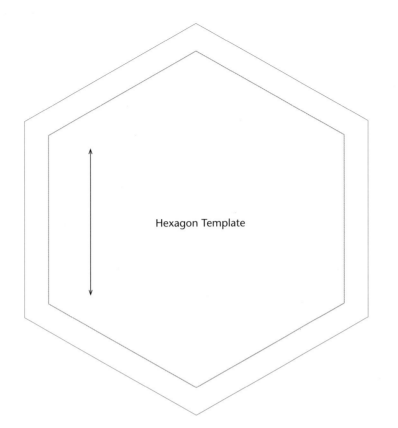

Hexagon Template

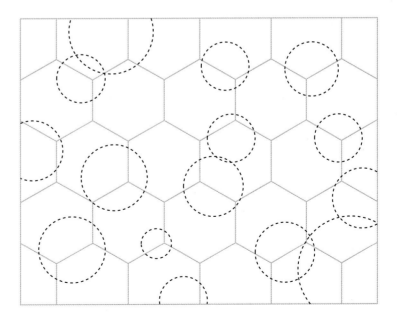

Quilting Suggestion

Jewel In the Charm

WILLIAMSTON, MICHIGAN, 1992

1600 DIAMONDS, 80 X 92 INCHES

HAND PIECED AND HAND QUILTED

ERRY IS AN ATTORNEY with a thriving private practice, a husband and two small children. She finds quilting a welcome escape from her busy daily schedule, and has produced a surprising number of quilts considering she does mostly hand piecing and hand quilting! Terry prefers handwork because it is relaxing and allows her to spend time with her family while working on her projects. A tribute to Terry's skill is her quilt *Christmas Nosegay* on the cover of *Traditional Quiltworks* magazine (January, 1996).

She dabbled in quiltmaking as a little girl, but it was a box of old *Quilter's Newsletter* magazines, sent by her grandmother, that fired her imagination. The magazines provided a welcome link to feminine pursuits that Terry, a second year law student, found missing in the masculine surroundings of Washington and Lee Law School. Because her grandmother lived across the country in California, Terry didn't see her often during childhood. The gift of magazines grew into an exchange of fabrics and other quilting goodies through the mail, a quilt link that provided a treasured relationship with her grandmother.

Terry was a member of the first two charm groups. She removed most of the lights from the fabrics gathered during those exchanges, and added jewel tones from her own collection. When she looks at this quilt, Terry sees a scrapbook of memories: a Vermont vacation that included fabric shops, friends who gave her pieces of fabrics, and scraps that were left over from a baby quilt made for her son.

Inspiration for this quilt came from Jinny Beyer's book, *The Scrap Look*. At the time *Jewel in the Charm* was being made, Terry had a design wall in a spare bedroom where she placed all the diamonds. Although most of the quilt is set as *Baby Blocks*, some areas merge into stars and the setting tends to change perspective as you view it. The diamonds spent two years on the design wall, where she would walk by and arrange fabrics when the mood struck. Sometimes her husband John would try his hand at fabric placement too.

Terry hand pieced the entire top by piecing small areas of the quilt and then putting them back on the wall. During the piecing process she still re-arranged the unsewn fabrics until all the piecing was completed.

DIRECTIONS FOR *Jewel in the Charm*

1. See pages 23–26 for set-in piecing. The example is made from the diamond shape used in this quilt. Remember to carefully place your darks, mediums and lights. Switching their order will change the perspective in the quilt.

2. When the top has been pieced, trim the top, bottom and sides to straighten the edges.

3. Layer with batting and backing and quilt.

QUILTING SUGGESTION
Terry outline-quilted each diamond.

Step 1

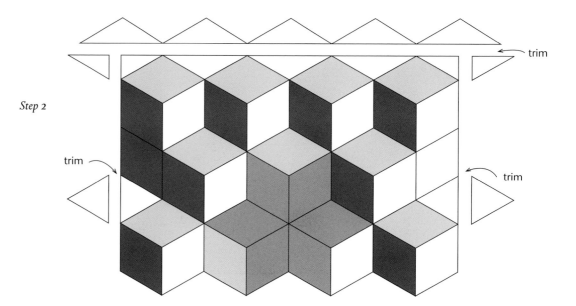

Step 2

trim

trim

trim

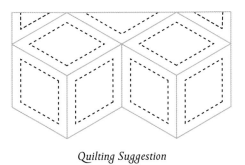

Quilting Suggestion

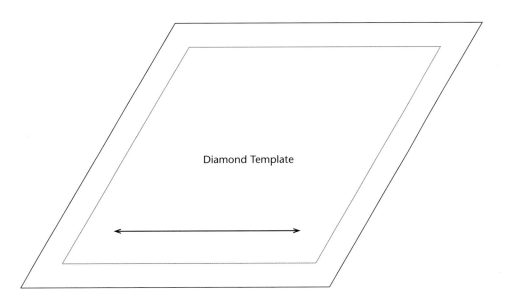

Diamond Template

Charming Possibilities

LANSING, MICHIGAN, 1992

929 HALF-HEXAGONS, 71 X 95 INCHES

HAND PIECED AND HAND QUILTED

 ACKIE COMES FROM a long line of quilters. Some of her earliest memories are of visits to her grandmother's house, where Grandma and her sisters (she was one of seven sisters; do I feel a quilt coming on?) would gather around the quilting frame. Jackie's mom also quilts. Jackie mastered many crafts while in her twenties, especially cross-stitching, but once she started quilting, other crafts fell by the wayside.

Jackie exchanged fabrics with ladies whose names she found in the Quilter's Exchange column of *Quilter's Newsletter Magazine*. She joined the *Daughters of Charm* group and enjoyed the variety of quilters, including new quilters who provided contemporary fabrics, and long time quilters who brought in the oldies but goodies.

Charming Possibilities is Jackie's first full-size quilt and her first attempt at both set-in piecing and hand piecing. Jackie never thought she would enjoy hand piecing, but she found it very portable and surprisingly fast. The successful completion of this quilt has given her confidence to take on new quilt challenges.

Jackie was inspired by the same *Quilter's Newsletter Magazine* article by Cuesta Benberry that fascinated me. She chose to piece the half-hexagons into units commonly known as *Inner City* blocks. Jackie remembers most of the quilts made by her family were very color-coordinated, so working on this charm quilt provided a real challenge. She wanted the center of the quilt to be yellow, so she pieced those units first. Then she used a color wheel to help her lay out the other units. She brought units to work and stitched them together at an outdoor picnic table during her lunch break, and was pleasantly surprised by the number of people who stopped to talk about her project.

Jackie did a terrific job. The yellow blocks give the quilt a central glow, while careful placement of dark, medium and light values insure stunning three-dimensional effects. The edges were finished with dark half-hexagons, and the top and bottom were trimmed. After a dark border was added, an isolated series of half-hexagons completed the top.

I'm especially impressed by the quilting design she chose, borrowed from fellow guild member Pauline Chute. Simple straight lines combine for striking effects that are carried into the border of the quilt.

DIRECTIONS FOR *Charming Possibilities*

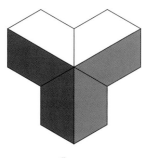

Step 1

1. Trace and cut the templates and fabrics as described on page 20, following the procedures used in the diamond sample (pages 24–26). Lay out the fabrics to make *Inner City* units. Pay careful attention to the placement of darks, mediums and lights. Press from the back in a clockwise or counter-clockwise direction.

2. Sew zigzag set-in seams to stitch the units together. Extra half-hexagons will even the sides. Trim the top and bottom to even the edges.

3. You may wish to add borders. Layer with batting and backing to prepare for quilting.

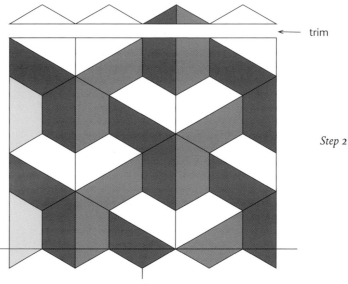

trim

Step 2

center

Jackie, who hand pieced her quilt top, used the unit construction described on page 76. I prefer machine piecing and am always looking for a short cut. As I laid out half-hexagons, pyramid shapes emerged. From working on samples of Debra's and Cindy's quilts, I learned pyramids are pieced with no set-in seams. By set-in piecing the half-hexagon shapes into pyramids first, you can straight-line piece the rest of the top. This is great if you are working on a design wall and have all your pieces arranged for the entire quilt before you sew. However, if you want to sew many units by color and then play with the placement of whole units, don't try it this way. Jackie's method is easier for keeping colors and values in place, but trickier to piece. My method is easier to piece, but trickier to maintain the order and values of the colors!

QUILTING SUGGESTION
A simple, stunning star shape appears by drawing a line diagonally across the half-hexagon, and another line from the starting point to the half-way mark at the bottom of the half-hexagon.

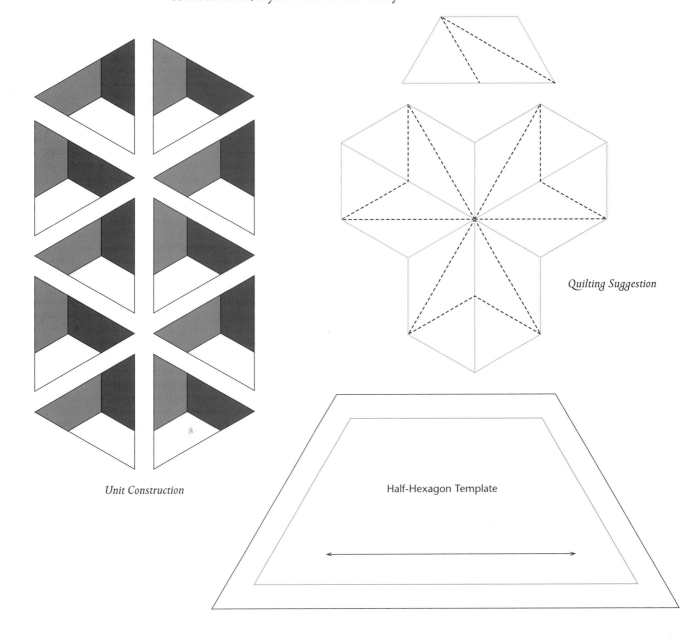

Quilting Suggestion

Unit Construction

Half-Hexagon Template

Charm Daughter

EAST LANSING, MICHIGAN, 1992

768 KITES, 69 X 98 INCHES

MACHINE PIECED AND HAND QUILTED

COLLECTION OF CATHERINE ANNE MUELLER

LOUISE MUELLER is the grand champion of Lansing area charm quilters. She has made ten charm quilts so far, using many different shapes, and always seems to have one under construction!

Louise's expertise is not limited to charm quilts. Her mother began quilting during her retirement and then introduced it to Louise in 1978. As a member of many small groups, Louise takes "orphan blocks" from friends and turns them into quilts for critically ill children for our local hospital (a guild-sponsored project).

Louise recently retired from her career as a phlebotomist (a person who draws blood for tests). She found quilting to be "an opportunity to stick a needle into something that didn't yell ouch!" She has made many quilts for family members, and each of her seven grandchildren has his or her own "Nana blanket." *Charm Daughter* is a gift to her daughter, Catherine Anne Mueller.

Using a pattern from Jinny Beyer's book, *The Scrap Look*, Louise found the piecing to be fast, but the hand quilting took a long time. She pieced the kite shapes into hexagon-within-hexagon units.

Louise is well known for her blue and red quilts. This quilt is an excellent example of her style and fabric collection. As the units were pieced, she kept the blues and the reds on the outside edges of the units, then added a few rings of light (gray) and dark (black) and an occasional green to provide contrast among the rings. It is hand quilted using an ingenious, straight-line quilting design. To finish the edges and create a border, Louise drafted four different units out of red fabric, and used set-in piecing to complete the top.

DIRECTIONS FOR *Charm Daughter*

This unit consists of both straight-line and set-in piecing. Cut out the templates and fabric as described in set-in piecing (pages 24–26). Steps 1 and 2 can be chain pieced and straight-line pieced. Steps 3 and 4 require set-in piecing. Some color hints: choose one color for the unit, but two different values of that color. For instance, if you chose darks for the center ring, choose mediums or lights for the outer ring. This contrast enhances the hexagon-within-a-hexagon pattern.

1. Choose six kites for the inner ring. Sew three kites together, twice, and press as shown. Sew the final seam and press as a pinwheel center (page 48).

2. Choose twelve kites for the outer ring. Sew these twelve kites into pairs and press as shown.

3. Use set-in piecing to sew the pairs from Step 2 to the hexagon from Step 1. Press the seams as shown on page 25 for set-in piecing. Piece the large hexagons into rows, and the rows into a top as shown on page 81.

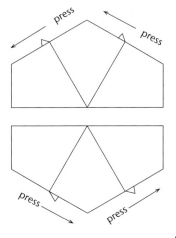
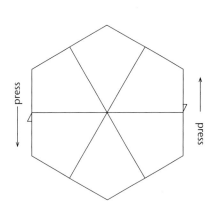

Step 1

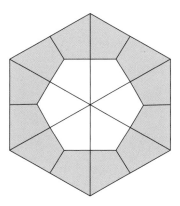

make 6

press →

Step 2

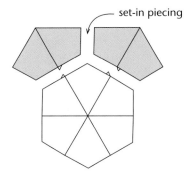
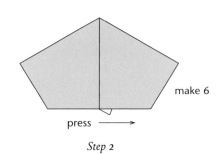

Step 3

4. To fill in the top and bottom, piece extra kites and trim as shown. To fill in the sides, piece extra kites. No trimming is required.

5. Layer with batting and backing and quilt.

QUILTING SUGGESTIONS
Like Jackie in *Charming Possibilities*, Louise used straight lines that combine to make secondary designs in the units.

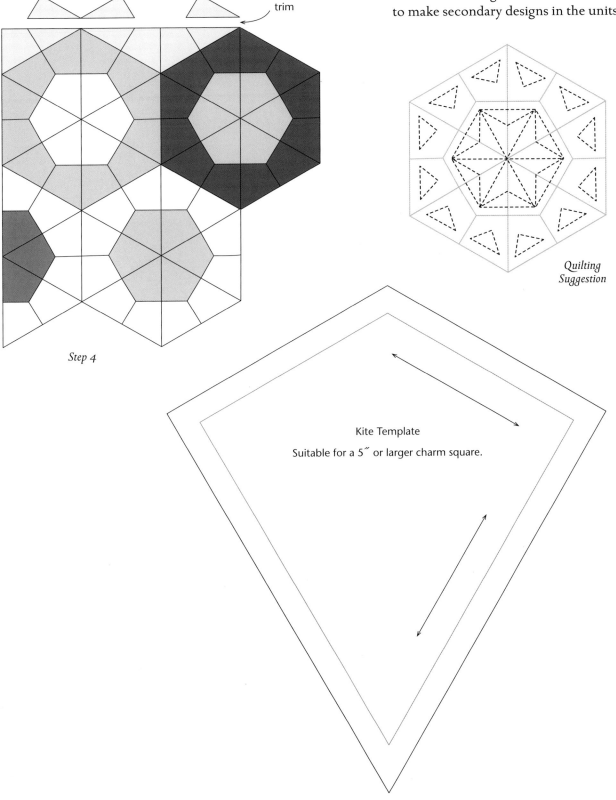

trim

Step 4

Quilting Suggestion

Kite Template
Suitable for a 5″ or larger charm square.

Scarlet Charm

EORGIA WAS THE ORIGINAL hostess and instigator of the charm hysteria that invaded the Capitol City Quilt Guild in 1988. We met at her house and she organized us all. She also managed to make this show-stopping quilt. Even though she has moved over an hour's drive away, Georgia still belongs to the guild, and is a member of the charm group that meets at Daisy's house, where the friendships have proved irreplaceable.

Georgia was inspired to make a Honeycomb quilt after discovering Linda Pool's quilt, *Francly Radiant* in Jinny Beyer's book *The Scrap Look*. Linda's quilt (page 35) uses a half-honeycomb laid out from the center, almost like a lone star. Georgia took the idea a step further and laid out the colors with the help of a photograph of an oriental rug. When she pinned the pieces to a sheet during the design phase, she found she needed many more reds. On a trip through a small New Hampshire town, her husband Jim bought red fabrics and she was pleased that not one was a repeat. In 1988 this was quite a coup!

After arranging all the fabrics on the sheet, Georgia began her first experience with hand piecing and was surprised at how much she enjoyed it. She pieced over a three month period, watching television with Jim. The piecing order is challenging because there is no straight-line piecing and the rows end up making huge diamond-shaped units with zigzag edges. Georgia sewed a few honeycombs together to make a row (or sometimes a partial row) and then replaced and re-pinned the row on the sheet to keep track of the pattern.

Because it is entirely set-in pieced, the pressing does not need to be done until the entire top is finished. As you sew, be careful to check regularly that the top is flat. When the design radiates from the center, there's a chance it might bubble. When Georgia was finished, she appliquéd the edges to a red fabric and added a striped border.

This quilt now resides on the guest bed. Next to the bed, Georgia placed a list of characters and surprises hidden in the quilt. Her guests are invited to search the quilt and look for the objects listed. Georgia's only regret is that she didn't include more novelty fabrics in the quilt and in the exchange. She feels these are the fabrics that make charm quilts more fun and visually interesting to explore.

DIRECTIONS FOR *Scarlet Charm*

This is a challenging quilt. The more I worked on the sample of this pattern, the more impressed I was with Georgia's efforts. Not only did she do a masterful job of piecing, but the design is set on point!

I suggest cutting and sewing just the center 24 honeycombs to test the pattern. This will help you decide on the size of your project. It would be a shame to cut 1000 charm honeycombs and find you don't like the techniques necessary to complete the quilt top! If you stop at 24 you can always square up the center unit and turn it into a charming pillow.

1. The illustrations correspond to Georgia's color layout. The units shown are for the center of the quilt. Cut and mark the templates and fabrics as demonstrated in the set-in piecing example on page 24–26. Use set-in piecing to make eight units, each with three honeycombs.

2. Use set-in seams to piece the eight units from Step 1 to make the center of the quilt. At this point, press the seams and make sure the quilt top is flat. You may press the seams in any direction, because all the seams are set in. If it doesn't lie flat now, it never will!

3. Continue adding rows to the eight sides of the quilt. Each row grows by one honeycomb. When you reach the total length and width you want, work to fill in the diagonals, where the rows decrease by one honeycomb.

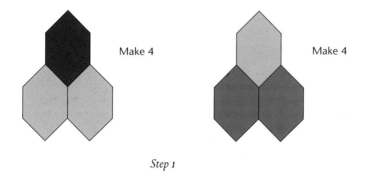

Make 4   Make 4

Step 1

Step 2

Step 3

4. Trim the edges to even the top, bottom and sides. Add borders if you wish. Layer with batting and backing to prepare for quilting.

QUILTING SUGGESTION
Georgia outline-quilted each honeycomb and chose a border from *Quilting Designs by the Amish* by Pepper Cory (page 78) that echoes the honeycomb shape.

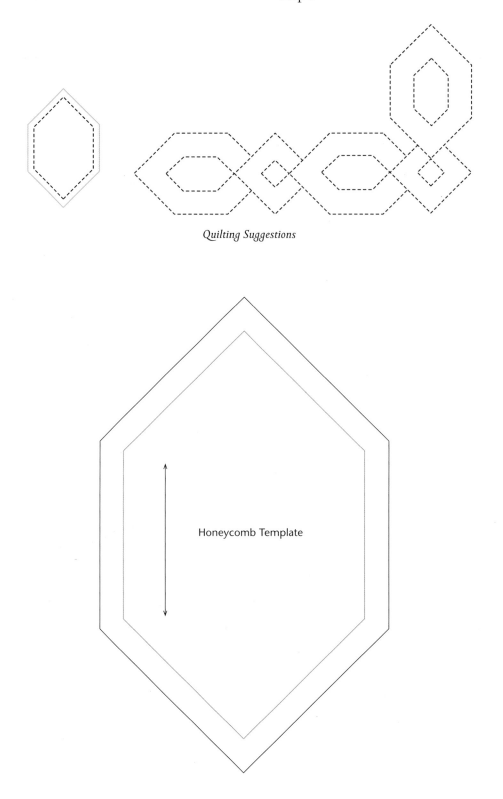

Quilting Suggestions

Honeycomb Template

Apple Core Charm

by Claire Ulasin

EAST LANSING, MICHIGAN, 1994

225 APPLE CORES, 45 X 49 INCHES

MACHINE PIECED AND MACHINE QUILTED

CLAIRE'S *Apple Core Charm* quilt is a sample she made to show fellow group members a charm quilt. She was inspired by a quilt made by Sharlene Jorgenson, on the cover of *American Patchwork & Quilting* (June, 1994). She loved the old-fashioned color palette and the plaid fabrics, and imitated this style with charm fabrics. She counted the number of each color Sharlene used. When she laid out the colors, she wanted more reds, so she replaced some of the apple cores with reds until the balance was to her liking.

The quilt was machine pieced in rows and then the rows were joined to make the quilt top. Claire machine quilted in the ditch with clear thread to complete the top. She likes to stitch in the ditch because she doesn't like the quilting lines to compete with the pattern. She left the edges curved and bound them with a straight of grain binding.

DIRECTIONS FOR *Apple Core Charm*

1. Trace, cut and mark the apple cores on the wrong side of the charm squares.

2. Pin well and sew an inner curve to an outer curve.

3. Continue sewing inner curves to outer curves to make rows. Press toward the inner curves.

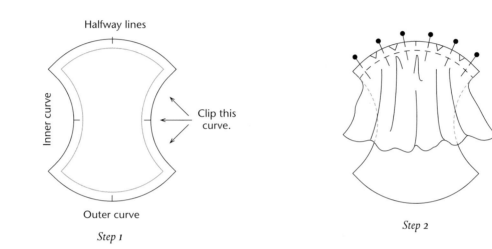

Halfway lines

Inner curve

Clip this curve.

Outer curve

Step 1

Step 2

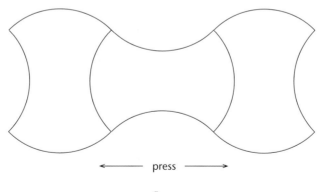

←— press —→

Step 3

4. Sew the rows together to complete the top. To keep the inner curve on top as you sew, turn the work over where the seams interlock. This is easier to do by hand than by machine.

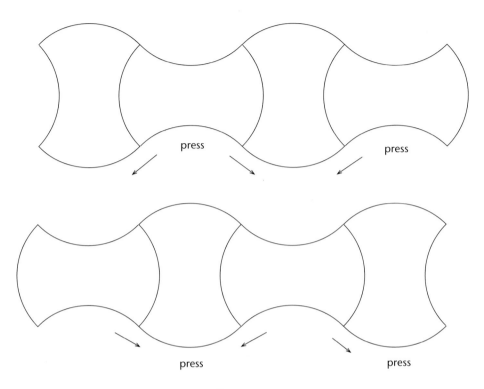

Step 4

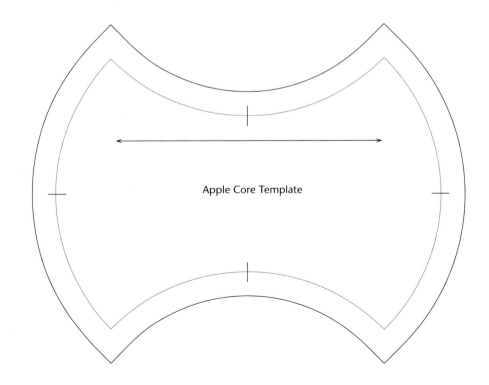

Apple Core Template

African Charm

by Don Worden

LANSING, MICHIGAN, 1995

256 CLAMSHELLS, 58 X 49 INCHES

HAND APPLIQUÉD. MACHINE QUILTED BY

NOLA HAINES, DIMONDALE, MICHIGAN

ON'S VARIED LIFE includes a Ph.D. in Clinical Psych-ology and a mid-life crisis that led to a law degree. A late-in-life career change found him doing tax returns to support his quilting endeavors. Meanwhile, his spare time has been spent in the pursuit of art, with classes in jewelry making, art welding and leaded glass preceding his interest in fiber arts. In 1988, Don noticed an ad in the local paper for quilting classes and signed up. He took tradi-tional classes from me, and then branched off to some free-form classes with Madonna Ferguson, where he started his African fabrics collection.

Don pursued art quilting through symposia featuring nationally rec-ognized fiber artists. He met many kindred spirits and his African fabric collection grew to include fabrics from Nigeria, Senegal, Benin, Mali, Côte d'Ivoire, Ghana, Swaziland and Botswana. The quilt has two hun-dred and fifty-five African fabrics and one tricot-backed gold lamé. When a local store that sold upholstery fabric went out of business, he found a lovely brocade woven in a clamshell design, just perfect for the border.

To lay out the colors, Don made a plan on paper showing the light and dark values. He chose the gold lamé as a radiant light source. A small selection of brightly colored brocades provided another focal point from which to radiate lights. The remaining prints were stacked according to value. Half-way through the quilt top, Don changed the orientation of the clamshells and used some circles to facilitate the change.

He chose to appliqué the clamshells while watching television in the evenings. When the top was finished, he trimmed the edges and added a thin border of gold lamé. It was then professionally machine-quilted in a clamshell design.

DIRECTIONS FOR *African Charm*

1. Transfer, mark and cut the template, including seam allowances. Make sure to include the half points to help line up the pattern while piecing (refer to Curved Piecing, page 27).

2. Clip the inner curve about 3/16″. Do not clip the outer curve.

3. To begin piecing, the first two rows are done simultaneously. Keeping the inner curve on the top, sew from the cut edge of the fabrics (point A), to the half-way mark on the outer curve (point B). Do not sew past this point into the seam allowance.

4. Repeat sewing clamshell 3 to clamshell 2. Sew from the half-way mark on the outer curve (point B) to the cut edge of the fabrics (point C).

5. Press toward the outer curve.

6. Continue building this row until you achieve the width you want.

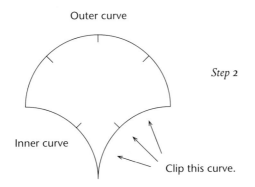

Outer curve

Inner curve

Clip this curve.

Step 2

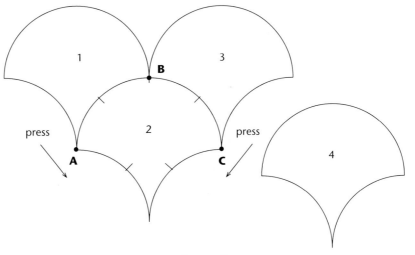

Steps 3–6

94

7. Beginning with the third row, piece the entire outer curve to the inner curves. Continue pressing toward the outer curves and add clamshells until the top is the length you want, or until you want to switch the orientation of the clamshells as Don did.

QUILTING SUGGESTION
This quilt was professionally machine quilted with a clamshell design by Nola Haines of the Quilting Barn.

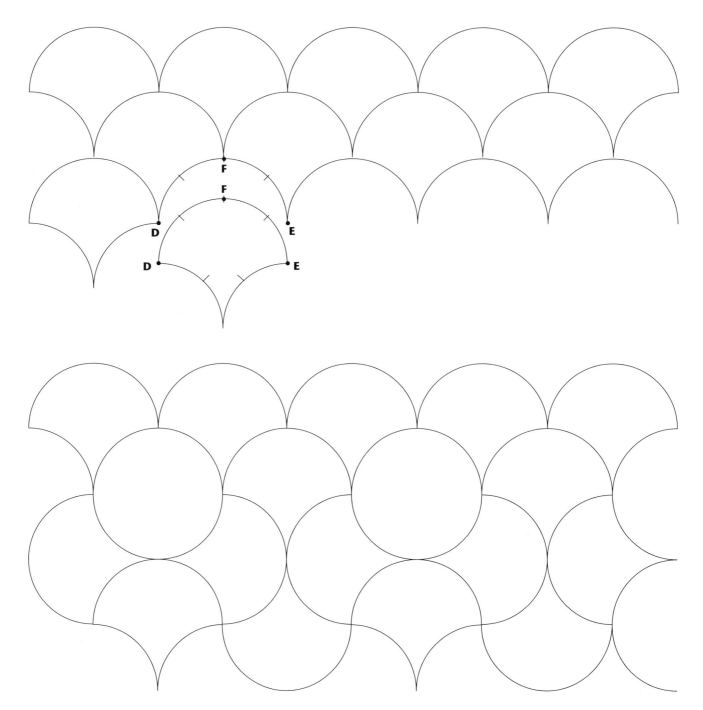

Step 7

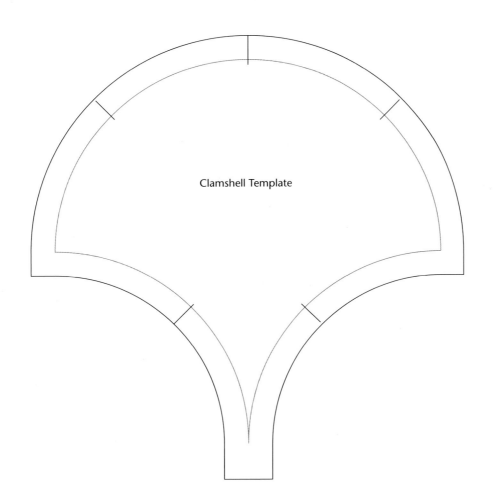

Clamshell Template

Clams Incognito

LANSING, MICHIGAN, 1996

180 CLAMSHELLS, 45 X 45 INCHES

MACHINE PIECED AND MACHINE QUILTED

*T*HIS QUILT was made to show off my collection of turquoise fabrics. I love the traditional layout used in the upper portion of *African Charm* (page 91), which I tried with blue-greens, blues and greens. The result was pleasing, but I was looking for something more unusual. I chose the layout found in the bottom half of *African Charm*, but played with the shading until I saw a curvy pinwheel emerge. I cut and sewed many turquoise pinwheel units, then added some contrasting colors to make the curvy pinwheels leap off the quilt. Having some of the pinwheels float over the borders helps highlight the pinwheel shape.

DIRECTIONS FOR *Clams Incognito*

1. Transfer, mark and cut the template, including seam allowances. Make sure to include the half points to help line up the pattern while piecing.

2. Sort the clamshells into stacks of four that are close in color, value and pattern scale.

3. All the sewing is done using curved set-in piecing (page 27). Clip the inner curves about 3/16″. Do not clip the outer curves.

4. Keeping the inner curve on the top, sew from the seam line of point A to the seam line of point B. Do not sew past the seam lines into the seam allowances.

5. Repeat sewing clamshell 3 to clamshell 4. Repeat twice, sewing clamshell 2 to clamshell 3, and clamshell 1 to clamshell 4, to complete the curvy pinwheel.

6. Continue sewing clamshells until you have enough for the size quilt you desire. Press all the seams toward the outer curves.

7. Arrange the clamshells on a design wall. Add a few high contrast curvy pinwheels if your colors are blending too much.

8. Since the entire quilt is set-in pieced, the order in which you put the quilt together is not important. I chose to sew the pinwheels in diagonal rows. An extra clamshell is needed at both ends of all the diagonal rows except the center row.

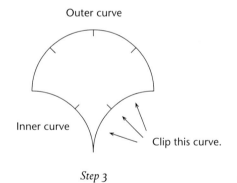

Outer curve

Inner curve

Clip this curve.

Step 3

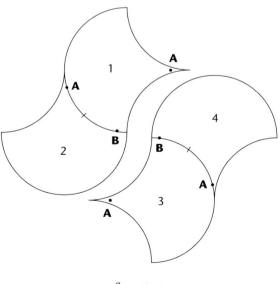

Steps 4–5

9. Choose clamshells to spill over the borders and pin them towards the center of the quilt top. Trim all the other clamshells on the outer edges to straighten the borders (remember to leave a $1/4''$ seam allowance when trimming). Add three borders: the first $3/4''$ ($1^1/4''$ cut), the second $1^1/4''$ ($1^3/4''$ cut), and the third $3''$ ($3^1/2''$ cut). Unpin the uncut clamshells and appliqué them to the borders.

QUILTING SUGGESTION
Layer and machine quilt. I machine quilted curved lines in the ditch and used the clamshell template to create the curved lines that change direction over the quilt top. On the pinwheels of different colors I used a modified version of the Papers Flying quilt pattern designed by Hari Walner from *Machine Quilting Patterns, Collection One.*

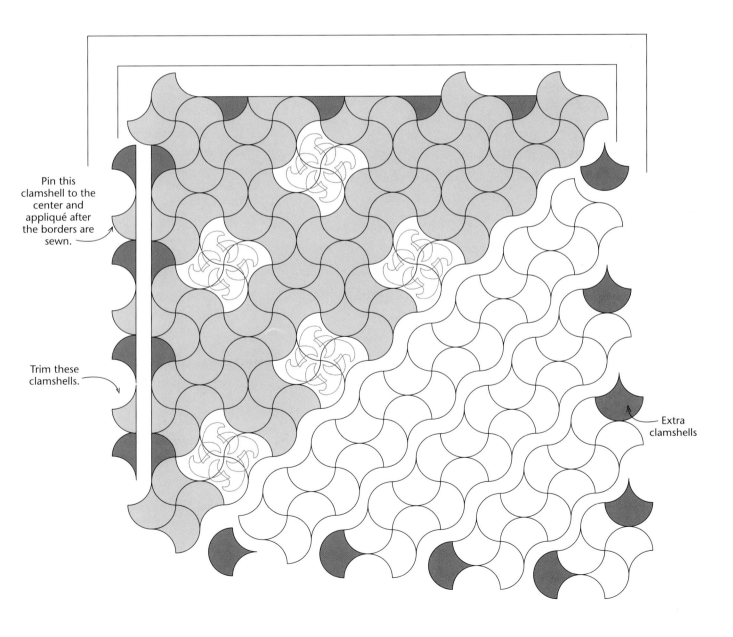

Pin this clamshell to the center and appliqué after the borders are sewn.

Trim these clamshells.

Extra clamshells

Quilting Suggestion

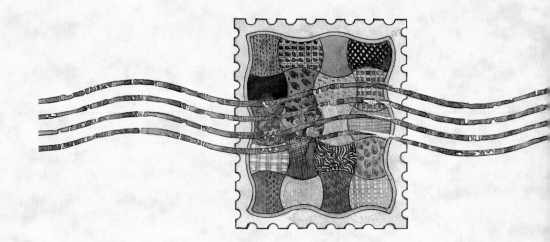

Part Four

RESOURCES

Resources

CHARM CONNECTION FABRIC TRADING CLUBS
1824 Morris NE, Albuquerque, New Mexico 87112.
Send a SASE for a brochure on six trading clubs with monthly theme trades and no membership fees.

THE COTTON CLUB
P.O. Box 2263, Boise, Idaho 83701   PHONE 208-345-5567
This fabric club now has three clubs. Twelve issues of 4″ samples for a total of 100 charms per year per club.

EZ QUILTING BY WRIGHTS
Wm. E. Wright Ltd., 85 South St., P.O. Box 398, West Warren, Massachusetts 01092
PHONE 800-660-0415
EZ Quilting by Wrights is a publisher of fine quilting books and a manufacturer of a complete line of quilting products and tools, including the acrylic charm templates for the quilts in this book.

PAT L. NICKOLS
P.O. Box 9607, Rancho Santa Fe, California 92067-9607
Pat's excellent paper on antique charm quilts is derived from an extensive data base. She is still documenting charm quilts, especially those made before 1950. Write Pat if you have information on charm quilts that could be included in her research.

QUILTERS REQUEST NEWSLETTER
P.O. Box 117, East Greenbush, New York 12061
A subscription newsletter devoted to swapping charms, blocks, fabrics, and more.

TRADER'S RESOURCE
72 Elmwood Avenue, East Aurora, New York 14052
A subscription newsletter devoted to swapping charms, blocks, fabrics, round robins and more.

Bibliography

AMSDEN, DEIRDRE. *Colourwash Quilts*. Bothell, Washington: That Patchwork Place, 1994.

BENBERRY, CUESTA. "Charm Quilts," *Quilter's Newsletter Magazine*. Wheatridge, Colorado: March, 1980.

BENBERRY, CUESTA. "Charm Quilts Revisited, Part 1," *Quilter's Newsletter Magazine*. Wheatridge, Colorado: January, 1988.

BENBERRY, CUESTA. "Charm Quilts Revisited, Part 2," *Quilter's Newsletter Magazine*. Wheatridge, Colorado: February, 1988.

BEYER, JINNY. *The Scrap Look*. McLean, Virginia: EPM Publications, 1985.

BRITTON, JILL AND SEYMOUR, DALE. *Introduction to Tesselations*. Palo Alto, California: Dale Seymour Publications, 1989.

CODY, PAT. *Continuous Line Quilting Designs*. Radnor, Pennsylvania: Chilton Book Company, 1984.

CORY, PEPPER. *Quilting Designs From the Amish*. East Lansing, Michigan: Culpepper's Press, 1985.

DUKELOW, RUTH. "Putting the 'Bee' Back in Quiltmaking," *Quilter's Newsletter Magazine*. Wheatridge, Colorado: April, 1995.

EISINGER, THERESA. "Picket Fence With Hedgerow Quilting," *Quiltmaker*. Wheatridge, Colorado: December, 1994.

GROELZ, BRENDA. "Ideas for Fabric Exchanges," *Quilter's Newsletter Magazine*. Wheatridge, Colorado: May, 1993.

JORGENSON, SHARLENE. "Apple Core, A Bushel of Plaids," *American Patchwork & Quilting*. Des Moines, Iowa: June, 1994.

NICKOLS, PAT L. "Charm Quilts: Characteristics and Variations, 1870s-1990s," *Uncoverings 1996*. San Francisco, California: The American Quilt Study Group, 1996.

WALNER, HARI. *Machine Quilting Patterns, Collection One*. Thornton, Colorado: Beautiful Publications, 1991.

About the Author

FRONT ROW, LEFT TO RIGHT:
Debra Mellentine, Phyllis O'Connor, Beth Donaldson, Ruth Dukelow, and Claire Vlasin.

MIDDLE ROW, LEFT TO RIGHT:
Jackie Beard and Norine Antuck.

BACK ROW, LEFT TO RIGHT:
Teri Nessia, Cindy Mielock, Ruth Farmer, Georgia Hayden, Daisy DeHaven, and Terry McKenney Person.

NOT PICTURED:
Louise Mueller, Mary Ellen Sample, and Don Worden.

BETH DONALDSON was born into a family where the sewing machine was always buzzing. Her mother, a proficient seamstress, specialized in Halloween costumes and slipcovers, while her sister was an accomplished sewer at age nine. Beth learned to sew in school when she was thirteen. After her marriage and the birth of her first daughter, she yearned for a break from home duties. Recalling a quilt she made in the 1970s, *Broken Dishes* (956 triangles, quilted through five layers of batting!), Beth decided to take a quilting course. She made her second quilt in a *Log Cabin* class taught by Pepper Cory. Since that time, she says "the quilting bug never let go."

When her homelife intensified with the birth of a second daughter, her quilt life multiplied as she became charter president of her guild. At the same time, she created items to sell at craft fairs to support her habit, and began teaching quilting in community education programs. In 1989, Beth co-chaired the Going To Pieces Conference, which launched the Michigan Quilt Network.

While she was teaching at the Country Stitches Quilt Shop in East Lansing, she began pattern writing and perfecting quilt assembly methods, which led to the publication of her first book, *Block by Block*, (That Patchwork Place, 1995) and her *Block by Block Pattern Service*, carried by shops nation-wide.

In 1990, Beth produced the Northern Michigan Quilters' Getaway, held in historic Bay View and featuring a nationally known faculty. Twelve retreats later, she is presently looking forward to a new challenge, as the Quilter in Residence at the Michigan State University Museum.

Beth lives in a suburban home with a first floor office-sewing room. She confides that "My daughters are busy teenagers, so my faithful dog Mickey keeps me company. My husband is very supportive of my home business. I am truly blessed and consider myself one of the luckiest quiltmakers alive!"